THE MATEJKAS

Also by Nancy Mowll Mathews

Cassatt and Her Circle: Selected Letters

Mary Cassatt

Mary Cassatt: The Color Prints

Maurice Brazil Prendergast, Charles Prendergast: A Catalogue Raisonné

Maurice Prendergast

The Art of Charles Prendergast from the Collections of the Williams College Museum of Art and Mrs. Charles Prendergast

Mary Cassatt: A Life

Mary Cassatt: A Retrospective

Maurice Prendergast: The Art of Leisure

Paul Gauguin: An Erotic Life

American Dreams: American Art to 1950 in the Williams College Museum of Art

Moving Pictures: American Art and Early Film, 1880–1910

THE MATEJKAS

*My Czech Parents Make
an American Life in Baltimore*

By Slava Matejka Mowll
with Nancy Mowll Mathews

iUniverse, Inc.
New York Lincoln Shanghai

The Matejkas
My Czech Parents Make an American Life in Baltimore

iUniverse books may be ordered through booksellers or by contacting:

iUniverse
2021 Pine Lake Road, Suite 100
Lincoln, NE 68512
www.iuniverse.com
1-800-Authors (1-800-288-4677)

Because of the dynamic nature of the Internet, any Web addresses or links contained in this book may have changed since publication and may no longer be valid.

The views expressed in this work are solely those of the author and do not necessarily reflect the views of the publisher, and the publisher hereby disclaims any responsibility for them.

ISBN: 978-0-595-46769-3 (pbk)
ISBN: 978-0-595-70508-5 (cloth)
ISBN: 978-0-595-91063-2 (ebk)

Printed in the United States of America

To Mother and Father

Contents

Introduction

Nancy Mowll Mathews

All my life I have listened to the best stories ever told about the immigrant experience in turn-of-the-century America. My mother, Slava Elizabeth Matejka Mowll, learned her storytelling skills at the foot of a master—her father, Jaroslav [Jerry] Matejka—and honed these skills as a teacher, and then as a classic American mother and volunteer in the post–World War II era. Through her stories, I learned to appreciate history as a drama of events small and large, human and global, carefully planned and maddeningly unpredictable.

My mother's Czech parents left the old country separately and first met on a boat heading to Baltimore in 1907. Jerry Matejka, whose father managed the forests of a nobleman's estate, was of higher status than Elizabeth was. She came from tenant farmer or peasant stock; however, they both had enough money and family support to travel halfway around the world to the grand adventure that was immigrant America. Their life together as "equal" Americans was one of hard work and personal volatility.

The couple raised their children, Jerry and Slava, outside of Baltimore in what is known as The County [Baltimore County]. They were the proud owners of eight acres of land near the shores of the Chesapeake Bay in an area that was rapidly changing from farmland to small businesses. Although Jerry Matejka was a Vienna-trained tailor, he saw the demise of hand-sewn suits, and he and Elizabeth developed a new business in retailing poultry and related farm goods. They enlisted the whole family in the buying of chickens from farms—now located increasingly farther from the city—and sold poultry and produce in a stall in one of the large fresh produce markets in Baltimore City.

My mother grew up in a city/country environment. On the one hand, she and her brother had the freedom of the wide-open spaces of Essex, but on the other, they made regular trips into the city for commerce. Her most vivid memories are of children's games that included even the chores, and of the abundance and variety of food from the countryside and city. The modes of travel from city to country, such as on a streetcar and in the family's wagons and trucks, loomed large in their lives.

My mother's identity as a Czech American was complicated. As a child, she made lifelong friends among the children of immigrant and non-immigrant families in her Czech neighborhood. Academically talented and boosted by the success of the family business, she completed high school and attended Goucher College, an institution of few immigrants. Eventually, she taught math and science in high school for nine years.

As a Czech, she was outraged by Hitler's aggression against Czechoslovakia that led to the Second World War. She was personally affected when her cousin Charlie was sent to Baltimore out of harm's way. Yet in 1941, she married outside of the Czech community and brought up her own family in the homogenous "American" style.

In 1994, I commissioned her to write these stories. Each chapter came to me monthly in handwritten pages over the course of a year. My mother was able to consult with her brother Jerry, who died the next year at the age of eighty-four. He provided many of his own memories and the bulk of the childhood photographs. His daughter, Lynn Matejka Gittings, helped them both facilitate the process, and she has been wonderfully helpful and supportive to me. Although I typed up the chapters and shared them with family members, the plan of publishing took a backseat to the art history books I have written over the years. Now my mother is ninety-three, and it is time to see her story in print.

Father in front of the new barn, ca. 1938

Prologue

We stood around the coffin in the living room that warm July day in 1943, exhausted from the long train trip from Texas. The Red Cross had sympathetically arranged a furlough for my husband to accompany me home after we received the telegram that Father had died after a painful seven-year bout with cancer. His thin body, straight and dignified even in death, reflected his dreams, his accomplishments, his struggles, and his many rebounds from disappointments.

He left his beloved Bohemia at age twenty to avoid compulsory draft into the Austro-Hungarian Army. He was determined not to fight for Franz Joseph, so he mapped out a strategy. He would go to America, stay five years, establish citizenship, and return to his village near the town of Humpolec where his father was a forester and where he, a slightly spoiled son, the younger of two children, was born. Disappointment number one: he was not able to save enough money to return in five years, and his mother, waiting anxiously for his return, lived only those five years. His father remarried and shortly thereafter produced a new son and heir. Father was no longer the favorite son for whom a loving family was waiting.

Anyway, Father had started his own family in the United States, and he was beginning to prosper. Years later he dreamed once again of returning, this time to a Bohemia freed of the Austro-Hungarian yoke, a land of milk and honey. Brother and I were excited about the voyage across the ocean to a country where chewing gum was unheard of, children were well mannered, athletic, and loved, and they all had grandparents! However something happened then too, and the trip was canceled. Brother's hoard of all flavors of Wrigley's gum became stale and brittle.

Much later, just two years into Father's fatal illness, he and I talked of a visit to the lovely, well-kept, carefully planted forest of Humpolec for one last look at heaven. Mother and Brother assured him they could handle the business so he could enjoy the trip and be my guide and host to the land of his birth. Disappointment number three: the winds of World War II were already blowing, and those who could, had already departed, or at least arranged for their army-aged children to leave. Poor Father would never again see his beautiful native land, which he had left temporarily thirty-seven years ago. But before he died, he found a creative way to console himself. When placed in his coffin, he had arranged to have his feet rest on a tiny tin box of Czech soil brought to him five years earlier by his nephew who, having been born in the United States was able to leave Czechoslovakia before the Germans overran the country.

Father bequeathed us certain values as our legacy: we would rather flee than fight; we accept disappointments but always look first for the creative solution, and we love the land—our own land. This heritage we pass on gently, like pieces of fine crystal, to the awaiting hands of those who will treasure it.

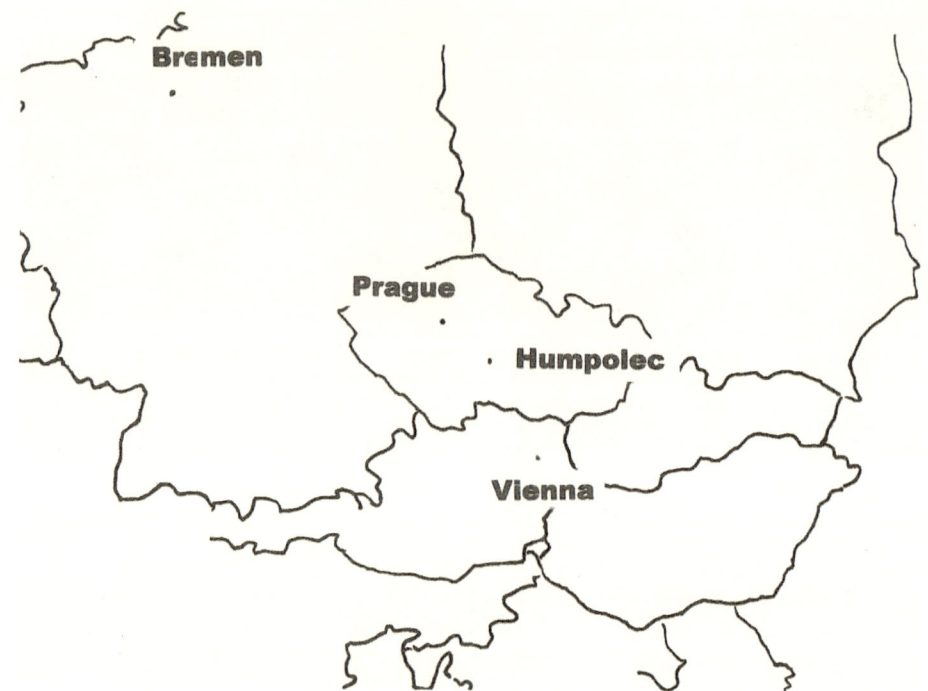

Chapter I:

Bohemia

Jerry V. Matejka (Jaroslav Votech Matejka) was born on April 13, 1886, in a forester's cottage on the outskirts of the town of Humpolec, the second of two children. It was a good life, being the son of the forester. On this huge estate owned by a nobleman, trees were carefully planted and tended, and mushrooms and wild strawberries grew abundantly. The nobleman taught Father at an early age to be on the lookout for people who carelessly destroyed new seedlings, cut down live trees for fuel, or started forest fires. Father went to the village school, took violin lessons, and escorted his older sister to local social events. "Gentlemanliness," knowledge, culture, and social skills were valued and developed. Father told me stories of his early entrepreneurship: making neckties from his mother's sewing scraps to sell to fellow students.

After eight years of primary education, Father attended the town upper school. There he lost interest in academic education and was quickly packed off to Vienna to learn a trade. He chose to be a tailor, following his early interest in making things of cloth. Life in Vienna was much more exciting than in the town of Humpolec or in the woods of the beautiful estate. In addition to his instruction in tailoring and later apprenticeship, he joined political clubs sympathetic to the breakup of the Austro-Hungarian Empire, became a dance instructor, and acquired a smattering of Austrian German.

While Father enjoyed the early trappings of culture and love and attention of a small family, Mother, Elizabeth Frances Zahradka (Alzbeta F. Zahradka) had a different upbringing. Born in 1889, she was the fifth of six children (two boys and four girls) of a tenant farmer. She was only a year and a half old when her mother died, leaving her in the care of two older sisters until her father remarried. That union produced another girl who became Mother's playmate. Unfortunately, this second loving mother died when Elizabeth was only five, and from then on, she became a little mother to her new sister. All four of the older brothers and sisters bossed the two of them while their father scratched a bare living from his allotted plot of land.

But childhood was a happy time. There was a fishpond on the acreage where the children doggy-paddled in summer and skated in winter (slid usually, since real skates were shared). Mother found school a joy. She was a good student, exceptional in reading and all kinds of fine sewing, embroidering, lace making, crocheting, and knitting. Her education ended after eight years. Her father died when she was eleven, and everyone was expected to be employed and help the family by the time they were fourteen or so. Under the wing of an older sister who worked in a laundry, Mother also got a job in a laundry. There, among the sheets and shirts with stiffly starched collars, she learned to iron beautifully embroidered handkerchiefs, pillowcases, and scarves, and I am sure she dreamed of having some of these herself someday.

The family soon broke up. Joseph, the older brother, heard that in America, anyone could buy land cheap and farm it himself, and soon he was on his way. James, the other brother, became a shoemaker, married, and then persuaded his bride to go with him to America where he, with his trade, could strike it rich. Mother decided to go with them.

As the nineteenth century ended, the United States no longer needed unskilled labor. The Transcontinental Railroad had been completed and mines and factories were bursting with laborers. But skilled labor was in demand, and so neither Mother's brother James (shoemaker) nor Father (tailor) had any problem gaining immediate entry. Single women, on the other hand, needed to have a sponsor, usually a relative who was already living in the states. Mother's sponsor was her brother Joseph, now the owner of a forty-acre farm outside Baltimore. So Father, age twenty, and Mother, age seventeen, packed their trunks in Vienna and Richlen (Bohemia) respectively. Strangers to each other, they both set out on different paths for the port of Bremen to board the SS *Rhein*, which sailed on July 11, 1907, for Baltimore. Father was full of his clever schemes for eluding the draft and making his fortune—all in five years. Mother was dreaming of a life in which the only embroidered handkerchiefs she ironed would be her own.

Wedding photo of Jaroslav [Jerry] and Alzbeta [Elizabeth],
January 10, 1910

Chapter II:

Baltimore

Mother and Father's shipboard romance is *True Story* fiction. My earliest recollection of it is pieced together from the joking conversations the neighborhood women had with my mother about her romantic courtship. These intriguing tales were usually cut short when my mother, feeling guilty about being away so long from her housework and the family business, took leave of her chattering friends. So I do not know if the neighbors were right and my parents really fell in love on the boat or if the romance blossomed in the social circles of Czech young people, which they both entered when they arrived in Baltimore.

Suffice to say that Father, who had planned to go to Chicago, stayed instead in Baltimore, where Mother's brother Joseph was waiting for her and where her brother James quickly set up a thriving shoemaking business. Some Czechs say that many of those who planned to go on to Chicago lost their nerve because they heard tales of fierce Indians in the Midwest. I prefer to believe that Father fell in love with Mother, if not aboard ship, surely very soon after they landed.

Mother was attractive, a good dancer, and outgoing. She first lived with her brother James and then with the wealthy Goetz family with whom she found a position as a maid. Father obviously admired the energetic young woman whose love of dancing and appreciation of the finer things matched his own. Father was also impressed with James' well-equipped shop and thriving business so much like the custom tailoring shop he was trying to establish in Baltimore. In the three years after they had landed, the two young couples, James and his wife, Marie, and Mother and Father, spent their time falling in step with a new world, different from the old one, speaking a strange language, but enjoying companionship and exchanging ideas in their mother tongue. How brave these young people were—adventurers all!

Czech Dance Group in Baltimore, ca. 1915. My aunt Marie Zahradka is
second from right.

Mother often spoke fondly of her arrival in the United States and how the
Czech minister of the local Presbyterian Church met them at the dock and
invited them to the Young People's church group—a lively helpful, friendly orga-
nization. Mother happily forgot her Catholic upbringing and joined this supportive group. They not only had good social activities, but also helped the new
immigrants find lodging and work, and encouraged them to attend English language classes to facilitate their assimilation into American society. They could,
however, take their time in this assimilation since Czechs and Slovaks and Mora-
vians—all "Bohemians" to Americans—could buy bread from a Bohemian baker,
meat from a Bohemian butcher, go to a Bohemian doctor and pharmacist, buy
engagement and wedding rings from a Bohemian jeweler, and read a weekly
Bohemian newspaper. Father was not going to waste too much time learning this
strange language since he intended to stay just long enough to establish citizenship and return to Bohemia.

Mother, however, jumped into learning English, signing up for night classes almost immediately. I write *almost* because first she had to find a job since brother James was not going to feed her for nothing. How many jobs she had and how long she kept them I do not know, but she talked fondly about being a live-in maid for the Goetz family—the Baltimore candy manufacturers noted for their caramel creams. In this family, she had the better of two worlds; she earned her own living and was encouraged to go to night school. She did very well with her English lessons since the eight-year-old Goetz daughter delighted in correcting her homework.

Father found a room in a Czech boarding house where the landlady made special Czech meals for her boarders, chief among whom was her not-too-ambitious husband. Father often spoke of how unprofitable their boarding house operation was with such an unproductive husband in residence. However, the food was good and several entrées accompanied each meal. Custom tailoring was a well-paying job, and Father became a custom coat maker for the Stern Tailoring Company and soon had his own tailoring and haberdashery shop at 1906 Ashland Avenue.

Meanwhile, Czech clubs and activities drew their personal lives together. Photographs of waterfront picnics reached by open-air streetcars showed large groups of men and women gathered to spend a day outside the city, eating, drinking, boating, singing, and dancing. In the winter, large group activities centered in the Workingman's Hall, the Sokol (Falcon) Hall, and the hall of St. Wenceslas Church and school. Each had its own band, bar, and kitchen and held special celebrations. The gatherings were all family oriented. Parents brought their children to the dances, and the little ones loved to slide on the outer edges of the freshly waxed floors. Older children tried dancing too. Soon the carefully wrapped little sleepy ones were placed on the surrounding benches leaving the polished dance floor to the adults. Czechs were good dancers, musicians, and gymnasts.

Sokol Hall was the training place for gymnasts starting at a very early age, and teams competed in all major cities here and abroad. This hall also was the center of a small Czech theater group.

The St. Wenceslas Church and school provided spiritual, educational, and social opportunities for Catholic Czechs and Slovaks. The smaller Protestant churches (Presbyterian, Moravian, Methodist, and Lutheran) looked after the spiritual needs of other breakaway Christians. The Workingman's group was "union oriented," and members quickly joined other groups in working for better wages and working conditions in factories and shops. The Sokols were the "Greeks" interested in a "sound mind in a sound body," and in personal freedom, and in the pursuit of happiness as one saw it. Since each group offered something special, immigrants had a good menu to choose from and to support.

On January 10, 1910, Jaroslav V. Matejka and Alzbeta F. Zahradka were married in the living room of the Goetz home on Broadway. Mrs. Goetz gave Mother one piece of advice: "Elizabeth, don't have too many children, they'll keep you poor." Mother must have thought very highly of Mrs. Goetz. Jerry and Elizabeth Matejka had two children who were wanted, loved, and carefully nurtured.

Jerry O. Matejka, ca. 1911

Jerry O. Matejka was born on January 28, 1911, at 1906 Ashland Avenue. The "O" in Jerry's name stood for Otto after a German friend of Father's who was a supervisor at the Stern Tailoring Company. Otto and his wife, Helen, a childless couple, often visited us after we moved to the country. I remember receiving a doll from Helen, and Otto promising Jerry an electric train, which never materialized. I do not think my brother ever forgot that broken promise and always hated the name Otto. He hated it so much that he had his middle name changed to *Thomas* when he reached maturity, and after he married and had a home and children of his own (two girls), he became a toy train collector. What long memories children have!

Nearly four years later, shortly before I was born, the family moved from the haberdashery store and shop on Ashland Avenue to a house on Decker Avenue. The house was new and on a wide street with trees planted in the center of the street, which gave it a country atmosphere. Here, Father, with Mother's help, continued to make custom-made coats for Stern Tailoring Company. Jerry rode his kiddy car on that quiet residential street and went to kindergarten.

The world, however, was not tranquil. With the assassination of Archduke Ferdinand of Austria on June 28, 1914, World War I went into full swing. On October 24 of that year, Mother and Father welcomed their new daughter. Mother wanted to call me "Josephine" after her favorite brother Joseph, but Father thought I should be named "Slava" (Glory or Gloria) to commemorate the impending breakup of the Austro-Hungarian Empire, and "Elizabeth" after Mother. Father, as usual, won, and Slava Elizabeth Matejka rounded out the family of Jerry and Elizabeth Matejka.

Mother and Father on their porch, ca. 1926

Chapter III:

Moving to the Country

Perhaps it was the treelined street or the ease with which one could buy and sell houses, but Father soon longed for a place in the country with trees and space and a stream, something resembling the well-kept estate where he had been brought up. Houses stuck together and trees growing in concrete and people everywhere cramped his style and dulled his entrepreneurial mind. Actually, he disliked being a tailor, tied to his heavy-duty Singer sewing machine, steam iron, and full-size manila paper patterns. Tailoring also employed my mother since her skillful fingers did the preliminary basting and small-iron pressing. This home shop had advantages, though, at least for Brother and me. A blanket on the floor in the room where Mother and Father worked became a well-supervised playpen for a crawling infant, and if Brother had a childhood scrape or bruise, he got immediate consolation from both parents. Work was plentiful, the earnings were good, and so dreams could become realities. Public transportation from the city to steel mills and shipyards and amusement parks made it possible to see some open areas surrounding the city.

So it was that in 1915 Mother and Father bought eight acres of land from the Taylor Land Company and contracted a builder named Hartman to build them a bungalow on the grounds—right on the #23 streetcar line, which went from downtown Baltimore to Middle River. The area, called Rossville, and later Stemmers Run, lay between Back River and Middle River on Eastern Avenue Road, an extension of Baltimore's Eastern Avenue.

When the house was finished in the spring of 1916, the family moved to their very own eight-acre estate. Father was ecstatic, Mother was appalled, Brother was disappointed, and I, age one and a half, had no opinion of the move. Trees surrounded the bungalow, Father's "castle" in the woods. No other house was anywhere nearby, let alone attached to it, and wild growing trees provided firewood, nuts, and Christmas trees!

Mother as Unhappy Farmer, ca. 1922

Mother saw things differently. Instead of a smooth dry concrete pavement abutting the front of the house as on Decker Avenue, there was a muddy path around the house. A lightly cindered driveway ran from the road across the street-car tracks to the backyard where the builders had brought in the lumber, bricks, and other materials for the house. The inside of the new bungalow was also less than perfect. The plastered walls and ceilings were rough—no finished coat ready for painting. But what could you expect for eight hundred dollars? After all, the house had four rooms and a closed stairway to the attic, a front porch with columns and railing, and a less decorative back porch. The roof was a good grade of tin destined to last for years. The attic was a great place to play, especially when it rained. I still love the sound of rain on a tin roof, but Mother had no time to listen to rain on the roof.

Her interest in rain was to watch it as it flowed from the roof into the gutters and down the rainspouts into rain barrels to use for baths and washing clothes. You see, we had a new bungalow and eight acres of land but no well. For drinking and cooking, Mother walked to the nearest well (a country block away) to fetch a bucket of water.

Father immediately set up his tailoring shop and continued making custom-fitted coats for the Stern Tailoring Company. In his spare time, he cut down, sawed, and split into stove lengths enough wood to feed the kitchen cook stove and the bedroom "chunk" stove. He often shot a rabbit or squirrel with his double-barreled shotgun, and Mother turned the animals into a tasty stew.

The parlor (living room) with an entry from the front porch boasted a pump organ, two or three strange-looking upholstered chairs covered with fabric in the summer and left uncovered in the winter, a mantel, and a round Queen Anne table. The parlor doubled as a fitting room for those country folks who wanted a custom suit made by a professional custom tailor—Jerry V. Matejka.

The fourth room very soon became the nucleus of Father's new project, the raising and selling of pedigreed chickens. He spent hours pouring over poultry magazines and plastering the walls of that incubating room with pictures of exotic, pedigreed chickens: Brahmas, Black Minorcas, Rhode Island Reds, Bantams, White Leghorns, et cetera. He would order a setting of eggs (fifteen to a setting) of a special breed, and using an incubator as a mother hen, attempt to produce a flock of special chickens, the eggs of which he would later sell for a good price. Of course, it was a risky business because if a setting produced too many roosters or the chicks died in infancy, the experiment showed no profit. I remember Father's beautiful letterhead that read, "Jerry V. Matejka/Pedigreed Poultry" with a picture of a handsome rooster and hen in one corner.

From the rafters in the attic hung full-size suit coat patterns of manila board from which various sizes of woolen or Palm Beach material were cut to make the coats Mr. Stern ordered. Spring and fall were busy tailoring times, but midsummer and winter were slow. This was when Father had time to develop his little "farm."

Czech farm magazines came from the Midwest. I particularly remember one from Nebraska called *Hospodar* (*Farmer*), which not only discussed farming and animal husbandry, but also contained a serialized novel for adults and a "corner" for children. We loved having Mother read to us at night by the light of a kerosene lamp and the warmth of the wood stove as we munched slices of Stayman-Winesap apples or nibbled the edges of freshly made chocolate fudge from a platter. No doubt, the fudge was for some special occasion like a PTA meeting, but Mother allowed us to eat the smaller "around the edge" pieces while we listened to her read the stories in *Hospodar*, in Czech of course.

Since Brother was five years old and had already spent a few months in kindergarten in the city (there were no kindergartens in Baltimore County in 1916), he enjoyed having another preschool year in Mother and Father's country school.

While there was no good, hard surface to ride his kiddy car on—a real disappointment—there were trees to climb, mud pies to make, storybooks to read, pictures to draw and color, and chores.

Before very long, Brother and I had a Saturday job. The display box of woolen swatches needed to be updated regularly. The swatches were numbered, and as that particular dye lot sold out, the number of the swatch appeared on a list sent by the manufacturer. It was our job to match the two, three, or four-digit number and remove that card from the swatch file. The swatches were large, as I remember, perhaps as large as a three-by-five-inch index card. Mother would then take those woolen pieces and make a quilt for the leather lounge in the big country kitchen. Nothing was wasted.

Very soon after arriving that first spring, Mother and Father set out to dig their own well with pick and shovel. No doubt, Uncle Joseph or some experienced "water witch" found a source of water with a divining rod, usually the branch of a peach tree shaped like a wishbone. He would hold the branch in both hands with the point upward and walk around until the tug of an underground source of water flipped the point down. And so it was that Mother and Father began to dig the well. Father dug and put the dirt in a bucket and Mother hauled it up with an improvised winch. After much backbreaking work, they had dug out enough dirt to put in one well ring, a heavy terracotta cylinder big enough to stand in. But that afternoon a huge thunderstorm struck and the dirt flowed back into the hole. I think at that point Mother picked me up, packed a few things, and left the country to visit her brother James and sister-in-law Marie who lived in a civilized city where women did not have to dig wells and mud was not constantly tracked into the house.

Mother had several relatives and friends who sympathetically gave her a place to lick her wounds and air her complaints. I loved these short excursions and the rides on the streetcars. What always remained a mystery to me was how Mother knew when to ring the stop bell on the streetcar when it was dark outside. "You ring the bell after Essex Avenue to get off at Ann Street," my mother would say, but Essex Avenue and Ann Street were equally invisible to me in the pitch-black night. Fortunately, I never had to ride a streetcar alone when it was dark, not even when I was six and went to school.

Somehow, the well was completed and even a little house was built over the pump. Soon, pumping water for our household and animal needs became another childhood chore. It must have been a good source of water because water has always been my favorite beverage wherever I have traveled throughout the world—even when we had to buy bottled water in Israel or France.

The Pump House, ca. 1921

We obviously all survived the first spring and summer and fall and Christmas, and even had guests from the city on Sundays. We heard the nocturnal call of the whippoorwills and imitated their calls in both Czech and English. Dishes were unpacked, tools bought, a small barn was built, and animals began to appear. A small dog was taught to sit up, shake hands, and follow wherever you went. A cat was allowed to live in the barn and catch mice, and oftentimes come to the back porch for milk and table scraps.

Mother walked to the store with a wicker basket on her arm. She bought bread and meat and canned milk and sardines, and other things a general store carried in those days, like kerosene for lamps and cigarettes and twine and brooms and clotheslines and frosted anise cookies and Eskimo pies. When the Fourth of July approached, sparklers and spit devils and rolls of caps and flowerpots and Roman candles and rockets appeared on special shelves at Josenhans' store. Then in August, those shelves filled with school supplies, notebooks, rulers, book bags, and companions (wooden boxes for pencils, erasers, pencil sharpeners, and pen points). Then Christmas toys, decorations, and special foods like nuts, figs, dates, and tangerines arrived. Josenhans' store had everything—even a slot machine where you could watch your penny zigzag along a crooked path and drop out of sight in the "no prize" slot.

Christmas was special. It came in two parts. The first event was on December 6, when Mikulas (Santa Claus) came and filled the stockings of all good boys and girls with toys and nuts and fruits and candy. Bad children got coal and switches in their stockings. All of our stockings hung by the window in the kitchen since, although there was a mantel in the parlor, there was no fireplace, so Santa had to come in through the window. How good it was to have a new toy like a gyroscope or a top or a tiny celluloid doll weeks before Christmas, and hard candy and nuts and a tangerine—that wonderful fruit even a child could peel.

Christmas Eve was the more solemn and dignified part, the night of the Christ Child's visitation. Somehow, in broad daylight, a fragrant pine tree from our own woods was magically trimmed and more and larger gifts appeared at its base. It was surely a magical time for a two-year-old, her older brother, and for their brave, immigrant parents who had moved from the security of their Czech community to live with country Americans daring them to survive and prosper. It was their challenge.

Brother and me, ca. 1921

Chapter IV:

Life in Essex

Many changes occurred the first five years of our move to the country. The government asked Father to make uniforms for the navy. Several Czech tailors did this. The pay was good, the work steady, but Father declined. He was a pacifist and wanted nothing to do with the war, even remotely. He chose to continue making custom suits (coats) for his regular firm even though he noticed two big changes. First, the quality of the dye job on the material declined and second, mass-produced suits had begun rolling off the assembly line. One whack of a guillotine blade cut many size thirty-six backs, fronts, lapels, or collars all at once. Any factory worker could now look like a banker without fittings and paying an exorbitant cost. No matter that ten other people wore the identical suit! It was a suit—coat, vest, and pants—at a price anyone could afford. But as custom tailoring slowly declined, there was still enough "bread and butter" work, though longer free periods, too.

The bungalow in the woods became home to gardens, fruit trees, a barn, a horse, a cow, several goats, even two pigs, and several brooder and chicken houses. Father enjoyed building these small structures and delighted in the outdoor activity. It was fun to go for a drive on a summer evening over an unpaved road beyond the streetcar lines. We could drive to the train station at Stemmers Run, Bengies, or Chase, and watch the trains, or go to a bigger country store and get special feeds or tools. We could visit Uncle Joseph and Aunt Bessie who lived seven or eight miles away and not on the streetcar line. We could go to "Uncle" Frank and "Auntie" Annie's house for a very special Sunday visit in midsummer by taking the open-air streetcar or a jitney to Middle River Bridge at the end of the #23 line. Then we boarded a launch—a large motorboat with long benches inside—to Long Beach where Uncle Frank met us with his horse and wagon.

Frank and Annie were special. They had no children of their own, so Brother and I became their children, too. It felt like having two sets of parents. Annie worked in a cigar factory in Baltimore all week and came home to their farm on weekends. Father always said Frank was the best gardener in the world; his vegetables were perfect, without bugs or blemishes. He sold the vegetables to city folk who came to Long Beach in the summer, or Annie would take the produce to her friends at the factory. Frank would not sell wholesale or to a cannery, that would be "farming," and he was a gardener. So Annie worked to pay the mortgage and came home on weekends to feast on fresh garden produce and have her loving husband wait on her.

Brother and I enjoyed the feasts and gifts showered upon us on special occasions. One of my four dolls—the one whose foot the puppy chewed—always got extra attention because Auntie Annie had given the doll to me. And Brother's stereopticon and many of the slides were viewed over and over. And what was our extra special dish at Uncle Frank's house? Succotash—sweet, crispy fresh corn fried in butter with freshly cooked homegrown lima beans. We did not grow either corn or pole lima beans in our garden because the plot at that time was only big enough for the little stuff such as lettuce, radishes, kohlrabi, carrots, and string beans. I remember when Father planted the fruit trees—apples, pears, peaches, and plums—and I kept asking when the fruit would appear ... like tomorrow? We had a hired man who worked for us occasionally. One Sunday morning while I was still asleep, he tied some ripened fruit to the branches of the little trees. I enjoyed the spoof ... and the fruit.

Essex School, Miss Morgan's Fourth Grade Class.
Brother standing second from the right, ca. 1919

Probably the biggest happening in those early years was Brother starting school. Since his birthday was in January, he had to wait until the following September (1917) to enroll in Essex Elementary School. The school consisted of two buildings of four rooms each, housing grades one through eight. Mother and Father agreed that school was important, that the teacher was boss, that you were to listen, study hard, and get "E's" (Excellent) on your report card. And if a Czech really wanted to get ahead, she had to be twice as good as the other student because she had a strange name and had to prove it was a *good* name. Mother was urged to go to PTA meetings, to make sure deportment was perfect, and studying was taken seriously. Reports from teachers were always good, and Jerry caught on quickly: avoid the roughnecks and the crybabies and stay safely in the middle.

Because we lived on a streetcar line, we usually had visitors from the city on Sunday afternoons. Mother would bake something special like apple strudel or kolacki (small buns with a filling of prunes and sweetened cottage cheese or poppy seed paste), which we served with an afternoon tea that was often flavored with rum. Often six or so folks would gather around the pump organ and sing Czech songs while Father played. Soon we owned a phonograph and many Czech records. The phonograph was a windup Victrola. We had lots of fun with it, especially when we did not wind it enough, and the song trailed off at a lower speed and lower pitch. Can't you hear the little kids giggling when that happened?

Children took turns entertaining, even we shy country kids. We learned many Czech nursery rhymes and were encouraged to recite them. I still remember the instructions voiced by the adults. *Hesky na hlas*, (nice and loud) and *Hesky Cesky* (in good Czech). These memory exercises stood me in good stead when I first went to school because I spoke *loud* enough to be heard. With Brother in school speaking and very soon reading English, and Mother reading to me in Czech and encouraging me to memorize and recite, I was soon bilingual, no doubt murdering both languages. I think I was born knowing how to count to ten in both languages. Well, maybe I was two or three years old. I also remember the laughter when "six" came out sounding like "chicks."

Entertaining ended before sundown when city folks went back to the gas lit streets and marble steps and sidewalks, and we would listen to the night sounds of the guinea hens roosting in the trees. We would then come into the house, light our kerosene lamp, and settle down to Father's puppet theater. The characters were actually small marionettes—china dolls with movable arms and legs activated by strings. They were dressed to represent good guys, bad guys, ordinary guys, clowns, et cetera. There was suspense, laughter, action, and rambling plots. Sometimes Father did not know how to end the story, so he said, "And then there was a paper floor and all the characters fell through." At that point, the curtain quickly dropped, the show was over, and it was bedtime.

Another form of entertainment was casting shadow figures on the wall when the first rays of sun came in the east window of the kitchen at breakfast time. With hands contorted, Father produced barking dogs, singing birds, and long-eared rabbits. How happy we were when we learned to do the simple projections ourselves. Mother was good with paper and string, producing cradles, hats, and quacking ducks. Then there were endless things made with flowers (wild or cultivated) like clover bracelets, necklaces, and crowns. We filled May baskets with fragrant wild Maryland magnolias or honeysuckle or lilacs. To this day, I cannot resist showing a small child the cute nibbling face of a bunny rabbit that can be found in a snapdragon blossom.

We also went on mushroom hunts throughout our own eight acres of woods. After an early summer rain, Father would take us into these woods to gather mushrooms. We each had a basket into which we carefully placed each edible mushroom, one Father taught us to identify. If we found one we were not sure of, we would take it to him. We soon learned that not all mushrooms were edible and some were indeed poisonous. Some days our baskets overflowed, and we proudly brought the mushrooms to Mother who relived our hunting experience by naming each one and complimenting us on our find. Then she sliced them, dried them in the sun, and carefully put them in white muslin bags for soups and stews she would make in the winter. Some she used immediately. I am not sure whether this one type of mushroom did not dry well or whether, because it grew in clumps, it was good to scramble with eggs and eaten as a meatless supper meal. I liked this dish better than mushrooms in soups. Maybe it was because I did not really like soup, which was always a first course of our midday dinner. Who could eat the main course of meat, rice, potatoes or dumplings, and spinach, cabbage, or carrots after a soup plate, and I do not mean a cup or small bowl of soup! Ah yes, the hired man could, but not a five-year-old child. Of course, we were taught to eat everything on our plates because some poor, hungry Chinese child would be glad to have that rice. How often I sat looking at that mound of rice (Mother always served rice by molding it in a cup first), and trying to figure out how I could send it to a poor Chinese child.

We were especially food conscious in those days. In 1917, we entered the First World War and subsequently received letters from starving relatives in Europe. In 1918, the flu epidemic hit. By the time Brother started school in 1917, we were already actively involved in the war, and heavy industry was booming. Shipyards and steel mills needed workers, and workers needed places to live. Towns like Sparrows Point, where Bethlehem Steel was located, brought in portable houses and expanded into suburban Dundalk. Dundalk, more carefully laid out and built, was intended to be the Roland Park (Baltimore City's finest residential area) of Baltimore County. At the same time, Rolling Mill (now Eastern Stainless Steel) was absorbing the town of Essex. Several blocks of prefabricated houses arrived, and suddenly the eight-room school was overcrowded and needed its own "portables." But wars cost money, so the working man was asked to buy war bonds and schoolchildren bought war stamps. Brother bought weekly stamps, one for him and one for me—our first patriotic gesture, albeit supported by our parents.

It was about that time (1917–19) that Father decided people were not always going to need custom suits, but they were always going to need food. So he rented a stall in North East Market in Baltimore City to sell chickens, eggs, and vegetables. The market was open on Tuesdays, Thursdays, and Saturdays. I am not sure how long Father's dual jobs of tailoring and chicken marketing lasted—probably less than a year—before he had to give up the stall. He decided to return full-time to tailoring to accumulate a nest egg, and at the same time, he was busy enlarging his poultry raising facilities.

Feeding the chickens, ca. 1922

Before I started school, I remember going with Father to Baltimore twice, once to deliver his custom-made coats, and once to buy chickens. The first time we took the streetcar. It was a pleasant adventure sitting by the window with my father beside me, just the two of us, taking this hour-long trip. On the way home, we stopped at a drugstore that had a soda fountain, and my father allowed me to have anything I wanted. I ordered a peach sundae with a cherry on top. About halfway through the beautiful concoction, I suddenly could not eat any more. My father waited patiently to see whether I really was finished and then he suggested we leave for home. By the time we got to the trolley stop I was wishing I could go back and finish my sundae, but alas, it was too late. Moral: next time get your ice cream in a cone so you can take it with you.

The second time I went to Baltimore we went in our wagon. We had to leave very early, like 5:00 AM, to go to the wholesale market on Pratt Street to buy some chickens. Mother gave me a blanket to wrap myself in just in case the early morning breeze was too cool for a little girl. Although I was well dressed for the trip, I soon found myself snuggling into the blanket and warming my hands by the wagon's lantern. The return trip was more pleasant. By then the sun was rising, and I was happily clutching a bag of my favorite candy, jellybeans, all mine. I do not know why it meant so much to me to have my very own bag of candy because I soon tired of the candy as I did of the sundae. I suppose there was something very special about doing something or going somewhere alone with my father. He always let me choose something just for myself. Today this is called quality time. Father knew how to give this time to me when I was five!

During the war, letters came from one of Mother's sisters and from Father's sister telling how difficult it was to get enough food. I remember the packages Mother and Father got together, items like rice, barley, lentils, coffee, tea, canned meat, and always a bag of candy for the children because "children don't understand war," my father said.

Then there was the flu epidemic of 1918 right here in our own city. People were dying like flies, my parents said. Morticians could not embalm the bodies fast enough, and caskets lined the sidewalks in front of funeral establishments. Saddest news of all was the death of our Czech pharmacist who worked day and night making medicine for the sick and then, weakened by so little rest, caught the flu himself. He left two young sons and his wife, Mamie, who knew nothing about running a drugstore. Since her brother was a doctor, he quickly hired a part-time pharmacist and supervised the business himself until Mamie could take over and give the business some semblance of continuity. Mamie had studied opera and never dreamed she would have to support her sons by tending the store, but with family support, she kept that pharmacy operating until both sons were educated. Both became lawyers. One son was named Wilson after President Wilson who was instrumental in the formation of the new Czechoslovakia, now free from the Austro-Hungarian Empire. During the flu epidemic, my parents were glad they were living out in the country where the pace was slower, where people were not jammed together, and trees filtered the air.

True, the country life had its drawbacks. The pigs caught cholera so could not be raised in our area anymore; one cow could not provide milk forever without "being freshened," and it was cheaper to buy milk than feed a pregnant cow for nine months. Goats ate more young fruit trees and expensive shrubs than we could afford to plant. Even the horse had to be fed when he was not working, so the big animals had to go. Jerry Matejka's eight acres gradually evolved into a poultry farm.

"The Old Gang." Mildred Habicht, Frank (Buddy) Habicht, Jerry, and me, ca. 1922

Chapter V:

After the War

When the dust had finally settled after the war, the world was different, even our little world in the country. Two new houses were built across the road from us. The occupants had been our neighbors in the city, and they wanted breathing space. I remember only vaguely this older couple with two grown sons living at home. The younger son, Frank, was a fireman, and he came to our house to help my father hitch up an uncooperative horse. It was a new horse, hard to handle, and this young, strong fireman was used to handling powerful horses. He also suspected that the new horse had been drugged a little to make him seem younger and more active than he really was. This was probably true because after a week or so, Father had no trouble hitching up this horse, which was not noted for speed. Later, when we bought our first half-ton Ford Model T, I remember Frank also came over to help crank the engine when Father was exhausted from the effort. "Ah youth," my father always said in Czech, grateful and appreciative of neighborly help.

Four children, five on weekends, occupied the other house across the street, so we had new playmates. Back off the main road lived the Czech shoemaker's family of four or five children. Two were Brother's age and two were older. On the corner of Essex Avenue and Eastern Avenue, was a blacksmith's shop, a great place for a group of children to gather and watch Mr. Leary shoe a horse, or watch sparks fly from the anvil when he pounded a hot horseshoe. If we were good and listened when he told us to stay away from the fire or a horse that may kick, he gave us an old horseshoe that the older boys used for pitching. We ran around in packs playing games, running errands, doing chores, and checking in at the house when we were hungry or thirsty. The community was ours; one long square block bounded by Josenhans' store on one end and Leary's blacksmith shop on the other, and in between, houses with children.

We enjoyed a carefree, fun-filled childhood. I remember some of the games we played, all of us—boys and girls, large and small. There were Duck on a Rock, I Spy, and Kick the Can, a variation of Hide and Seek. The game went like this. Instead of counting to give the players time to run and hide, the "It" person ran to retrieve a can that a "strong" kicker had kicked off a base. The "It" person brought the can back, and then looked for the others who were by now out of sight. When "It" spied someone he would say, "Buddy behind the bush!" and hit the can three times. If, however, "It" had to wander too far from base, a hider could run in from his hiding place and call "in free!" if, of course, he beat "It" to the base. This was a favorite game to play at dusk. It was loud enough, with short pauses of contrasting quiet to let our parents know where we were.

An interesting game always played in broad daylight and always at our house, used a soft rubber ball the size of a baseball. The game was called, Andy Over. We chose sides and then we lined up at the front and back of the house. One of the players would throw the ball over the roof and call "Andy!" When the other side saw the ball, now rolling down their side, they would yell "Over." If someone on that side caught the ball, the players would run around the house and catch as many players as they could before they could run around the house to their own side again. If the ball was not caught, there was no running and capturing, but the ball was put into play by throwing it back over the roof and yelling "Andy!" again, giving the other side a turn to catch and capture. Since the turns proceeded down the line of children, there were frequent calls of "Andy" with no corresponding "Overs." Not too many children had the skill and strength to get a ball over the roof. The game ended when all players were captured, the ball was lost, someone had to go home, or my parents could not stand the sound of a ball hitting the tin roof one more time.

There were quieter games and games that were more individual too, like marbles and hopscotch. There were also seasonal activities like sledding or gathering whatever was good to eat at that time of year. In the spring, dandelion blossoms were gathered (for dandelion wine), or dandelion greens or pokeweed gathered for early spring greens cookery. In the summer, we picked wild strawberries, blackberries, and huckleberries (wild blueberries). In the fall, we gathered chinquapin and hickory nuts, and for winemaking, elderberries. With new neighbors all around, families often swapped recipes, but successes and failures in cooking, baking, or winemaking usually remained family secrets.

Often Mother and Father encouraged us to sell our blackberry and huckleberry pickings to the local store. Mrs. Josenhans always paid us top price for our berries, and Father put our earnings into his "bank" along with our "pay," which we got when we did work for him. He kept good records, obviously made good investments with "our" money because, when the Essex branch of the Overlea bank opened early in the 1920s, he paid us what we had in his "bank," and we opened savings accounts in a real bank. My account showed a deposit of forty dollars. I think I was nine. The rule was that all earned money went into the bank. Father would not allow withdrawals. After all, didn't he provide for all our needs and give us ten cents to spend on Sundays, and money for movies, et cetera? Savings were to be used for something really big. But Father's "big" was never what I considered "big," like a bicycle. Finally, after being forced into the habit of saving and continuing this philosophy with my first full-time job, I used my savings for my first "big" investment—a green Chevrolet coupe with a rumble seat. I paid $550 cash for it. I was twenty-one.

I remember one "paid" job Jerry and I did for Father. While he was still tailoring he began to raise ducks, Muscovy ducks they were, a better breed than the popular Long Island ducks, which grew faster but accumulated too much fat. He decided his ducks needed a duck pond, so he set about digging a small one, which caught the water that drained from the orchard during rainstorms. He had enough free time to dig the pond, but not enough time to haul the dirt away. With the first rainstorm, the pond filled with water and the mound of dirt became a sliding board. Four of us kids discovered we had a tiny swimming pool with a mudslide. We have a picture showing us on top, ready to slide into the muddy water. What fun! Then Jerry and I hauled the dirt away in our "express" wagon at three cents per load. He got two cents and me, I got one cent. Father paid us immediately after each load.

At the back porch, ca. 1921

During this time, half of the back porch, the part leading into the kitchen, had been screened to keep flies out of the kitchen, and also away from crocks of fermenting pickles or wine or other foods in various stages of preparation on that part of the porch. Father's sewing machine was at the window facing the porch. To keep us from distracting him while he was sewing, he rigged up a cardboard chute from the top of his machine and out the bottom of the window. When we had moved a wagonload of dirt, we went on the screened porch to the "pay window," and down the chute came three pennies with a cheerful note of encouragement from the paymaster. I do not remember how many loads we moved before we quit, but while we kept at it, there were long periods of quiet between slams of the screen door, and our parents knew we were doing something productive. Of course, this was before child labor laws went into effect!

One day Jerry went to Baltimore with Father to make a coat delivery, and on the way back, they stopped to buy an ice cream freezer. You had to buy a specialty item like this in a large hardware store in town. The freezer was too big to fit under a seat, so Father stood in the rear of the streetcar with his newest purchase and the conductor. Since it was summer, the conductor kept both doors open for extra air circulation. Going full speed down the hill from Crosse & Blackwell, the streetcar lurched and the freezer rolled out. "Stop! Stop! My freezer, my freezer!" my father called out. At the bottom of the hill, the motorman stopped the streetcar, took the steering control, reversed the trolley, and calmly sent the car back up the hill. They picked up the undamaged freezer and went down the hill again, a little slower this time. There was no charge for the extra ride and pick up. Those were the days of customer service, even on public transportation!

Thereafter, we made ice cream on Sundays—vanilla, chocolate, peach, and cherry—or we made lemon water ice. Mother made the mixture; Father crushed a block of ice in a burlap bag, and packed the ice with layers of coarse salt around the metal gallon container with the dasher and the fruit and cream mixture inside. Then he put the gear top on, and Jerry and I took turns cranking. When neither of us could get the dasher to turn in the newly thickened ice cream, Father would finish the job. We carefully removed the salty ice from the top of the container, removed the gear top, and lifted out the dasher with a generous coating of ice cream still on it. We all grabbed a spoon and took a first taste right off the dasher as a reward for our labor. Then Father put a cork in the dasher opening, poured off the salty melted ice, and then packed fresh salt and ice around the container to keep the cream frozen while it ripened. The ice cream would be ready to serve later that day after Sunday dinner.

Life in the country was a seven-day job, but Sunday was special. With the exception of feeding the chickens, ducks, geese, guinea hens, and our other animals, no one did any paid work on Sundays. Most of the day we spent preparing special meals, making baked goods, and preparing ice cream. Mother also used Sunday to polish her big brass bed. I have always hated brass beds … Mother did not need another job on Sundays.

Riverview Park, ca. 1920

During the summer, we would always save one evening to visit a small amusement park on our side of Back River, but we liked one of the larger parks better because we enjoyed the longer trolley ride in the cool of a summer evening. We liked the lights, the games, the rides, the music, and the excitement. We all rode the merry-go-round, our parents on the high-back seats and my brother and me on the flying horses. Soon we graduated to racer dips, caterpillar rides, and scary fun houses. Father would play the wheel until he won a box of chocolate cordial cherries for Mother. These were her favorite. He also got them for her when he had a good paycheck. We used the empty candy boxes to hold coins and large bills, and during slack seasons, our grocery bills from the "Bee Hive of Industry," Josenhans' store.

One of our neighbors operated a small lunchroom near Bay Shore Park where ferries docked after sailing back and forth across Chesapeake Bay. Once each summer, Mr. and Mrs. Rice would load six of us neighborhood kids in their new three-door Ford sedan and take us to their lunchroom for the day. They would feed us and let us wander around, but we had to make sure the older ones looked out for the younger ones. We watched the big Rock Hall ferries come and go, and then in the afternoon, we walked to the amusement park. I do not remember how far it was, but part of the way we walked on the seawall, which was very scary for me since I was one of the smaller kids. Our parents had given us spending money for the day, and somehow we made the money pay for a ride or two, and for cotton candy and peanuts. It was not like going somewhere with Father who was always available when your money ran out. Time at the amusement park was fun, and we all walked back to the lunchroom in time for hot dogs and the long ride home.

Mr. and Mrs. Rice, a childless couple, kept a flock of geese, which were better guards than most watchdogs. Whenever anyone walked in the long lane, the geese made an awful racket and the gander would actually attack with his powerful bill and outstretched flapping wings. I was always afraid to go into the geese yard alone and for good reason. That gander nipped me on the leg once while his flock loudly cheered him on.

Mother and Mrs. Josenhans became friends. Mrs. Josenhans asked Mother if she would teach her daughters how to do some fine needlework at which Mother excelled. So one afternoon each week during the summer, Mother would teach the girls how to embroider things like pillowcases and dresser scarves and linen towels. It was a pleasant change for Mother. She was an excellent teacher. In appreciation, Mrs. Josenhans gave Mother a subscription to *Needlework* magazine, which Mother read and treasured. She taught me needlework too, simple outline stitching, the cross-stitch, and even how to make French knots. By the time I was five, I had made a small, round doily embroidered neatly with a boy and his dog. The doily, edged in handmade lace, was a bit irregular, but good enough to save and admire as my first piece of needlework.

In the fall of 1920, I joined the hallowed ranks of children marching off to school. The walk was long, about a mile, but not a lonely walk because I started out with my brother and then others joined us along the way. If it rained, we rode the streetcar. The fare was four cents. Neatly tied in the corner of our handkerchiefs were four pennies for the ride home if it was raining again when school let out. Those pennies were not to be used for any other purpose. Even though there was a small confectionery store near the school, and a bakery that sold doughnuts three for a nickel and small pies for eight cents, we never, ever spent those four pennies for anything but a trolley ride home in the rain. Our parents did a good job of teaching us the proper use of money. I suppose we appreciated the comfort of not having to walk that long, tired mile home in the rain, and felt a certain security in that knot of pennies. No doubt, we lost them occasionally, but not too often. Mother always checked to see that we had everything before we went off to school: books, lunch, and the handkerchief of pennies.

We were never late to school, and Mother taught us to head straight home after classes. We came home, changed into play clothes, and then we could play or visit with our friends. We learned that you finished one job before you started another. School was our "job." It was also good to change into old clothes and comfortable old shoes and run into the nearby woods looking for ripe chinquapins, those small chestnuts in burrs that grew on bushes rather than in trees. We boiled or roasted the nuts on the wood stove and enjoyed both the hot nuts and the heat of the fire on nippy fall evenings.

Days were shorter as winter approached and there was less time to play outside, so indoor activities took over. Mother still read stories to Brother and me. She read from Czech farm magazines, and "Uncle Wiggily," and other comics from the Baltimore evening paper. Sometimes we played games like checkers or a special board game Father made named "The Mill," which used large buttons instead of checkers, and was a faster, simpler game. We played tic-tac-toe, which required only a piece of paper and pencil. And there was homework, even in grade one. Parents were to correct the items marked "X." Classes were large and children not promoted if they got too many X's on daily work, so parents were expected to help their children if they themselves could read and count. In that day, when a child repeated grades one, two, and three at least once, the child often became discouraged, and since the student was also much older than the regular classmates were, the child often quit school. At that time, some adults even bragged about having only gone through the third grade, and they were doing okay. Health was another deterrent for some children. The schools had yearly physical and dental examinations. You got a white button to wear if you passed the physical and a brown one if you didn't. My very good school friend got a brown button. She had a heart murmur, but that heart was of gold. One friend said of Edna at her death fifty-five years later, "If Edna had a nickel, half of it was yours." Edna shared anything she had with anyone. What a tribute!

I remember three things about my first year of school.

1. I learned to say "six" rather than "chicks" because Mother's *hesky na hlas* (nice and loud) carried over into my recitations in school. If I told my mother that someone laughed at me or called me names, she taught me to say, "Sticks and stones may break my bones, but names will never hurt me." I learned many sayings like this in both languages that first year. Years later, when the son of my old college friend took a crash course in military Czech, I shared with him an old Czech grammar book I still had that was filled with the phrases I had grown up with. How different it was from the coarse military language he had learned!

2. I learned that "fast" was not always "accurate." Our first grade class was crowded. We sat in double desks, sometimes three to a seat. Sometimes two of us shared a box of "letter" or "phrase" cards. This day the teacher wrote five phrases

on the board and we were supposed to match them at our desks. My seatmate was one of those quick-study kids. She took one look at the first letter of each phrase and matched them that way. My slower, more painstaking approach would have earned us more credit, and I could hear my mother say, *Nic hulla bulla!* (Don't be sloppy). Now, seventy-five years later, I am still fond of the phrase, "Make haste slowly."

3. Because many families moved to our area during the war, and then stayed to work in the steel mills and shipyards and later the airplane factory, our school required more and more portable classrooms. Soon a bond issue to build a new school was on the ballot. I remember that schoolchildren paraded in Essex to get out the vote. Our mothers glued letters of the alphabet on crepe paper sashes. The sash I wore was blue with gold letters that read, "Vote for the Bond Issue." Six years later, our seventh grade class washed the windows in our huge new brick school, and raked the grounds and planted shrubbery. However, the following year, our eighth grade class moved back to the old building because the new school was already too crowded. And so it goes in a democracy. Today's parents must plan and work so tomorrow's children will enjoy the reality of our dreams.

Me with a streetcar going in front of our house, ca. 1922

Chapter VI:

The Fast-Moving Twenties

So much happened so fast in the twenties, I do not know how or exactly what to tell to make this story meaningful, true, and unique. Prior to World War I, it was an advantage to live on a streetcar line. If you lived in the city, (Baltimore) you could work in the steel plants or shipyards and escape to the country on weekends; or, you could live in the country and trade in the city. So I must tell you the story of how Brother got his bicycle. Father took him by streetcar to a bicycle shop in East Baltimore. They chose a red one, size twenty-six (a man's size was a twenty-eight) with a luggage carrier on the back. Then, with Brother sitting on the luggage carrier, Father pedaled the new bicycle home a distance of eight to ten miles. Father was young then, and his son needed a bicycle, a boy's passport to adventure, independence, and ownership. I didn't realize how personal and private this ownership was until I surreptitiously learned to ride his bike, and Brother, when he found out, immediately raised the seat so high that I couldn't reach the pedals. My parents softened this blow by getting me a scooter, which my new friend and neighbor also had. It was an acceptable peace offering, and Bertha and I had fun riding our scooters. But ... it wasn't a bicycle.

Living on a streetcar line also made it possible for Mother to go shopping downtown for dress materials in dry goods stores and for special foods and seasonal items found only in big city markets. I remember one such day in winter just before Christmas. Because it had snowed that day, the streetcar tracks needed sweeping, meaning the cars were running slower and slower. Soon it was nearly suppertime, and still no sign of Mother with all the groceries and stuff. Father was good at dispelling the anxiety that showed in our faces. He simply said, "Let's see what we can find to eat," and he opened a big lard can where Mother kept special baking ingredients. Father then fed us raisins, candied cherries and pineapple, almonds and filberts. We thought it was Christmas and soon afterward Mother appeared, and we *knew* it was Christmas. She told us why she was late.

There was a fire on the hill by the cannery and the streetcars could not get through. The cars coming the other way were stuck on the other side of the hill. So they unloaded the passengers, walked them around the fire onto the waiting cars, reversed directions, and got one load of passengers safely to their destinations. But that was the last car to go to Middle River until the next day when the fire was contained and a track sweeper could get through. Needless to say, we were happy that Mother was safely home.

It was nice to live on a streetcar line and to have a connection to trains going to Washington, Philadelphia, New York, Cleveland, and Chicago. We have pictures of our train trip to Philadelphia. Here we were all dressed up, going to the city where Czechoslovakia was proclaimed a nation. How proud the Czechs were of their new free country. Gymnast groups became active and held annual inter-city competitions. Drama groups gave plays, music groups formed, and bands played for outdoor and indoor festivals.

Brother attended Kaspar's Music School to take violin lessons. I remember watching Father and Brother practicing in the living room and wishing I too could be part of this music circle. But Brother's brush with violin lessons was short lived. There were too many other things to do, like playing soccer with the boys on Sundays instead of going to town to take a violin lesson. So Father gave up and instead, encouraged Jerry in his athletics—high jump, broad jump, and track events. How proud we all were when he won bronze, silver, and gold medals in the annual track and field competition held in Patterson Park.

Perhaps the biggest change in our lives was the appearance of automobiles in our yard on Sundays. It seems our Czech friends who owned stores were our first visitors who had cars after World War I. The Kozaks, who had two grown sons and a daughter, had sold their small grocery store in a Czech neighborhood and bought a larger store in a more affluent section. They were the first to appear in their new Dodge touring car. They not only visited with us as they had always done, but they drove us to the Druid Hill Conservatory and Zoo. Then there were the Nenadals who had a dry goods and a clothing store for children in Curtis Bay, who proudly showed off their new Nash. Locally, there was Mr. Habicht who drove for the Wagner Lumber Company. In the evenings, he often took Brother and his son Buddy with him when he had bills to collect. Brother was always ready to go when invited; cars fascinated him. He knew all of the makes and models by sight, and often sat on the front porch on Sunday evenings and kept count of all the different kinds of automobiles: Star, Ford, Chevrolet, Marmon, Dodge, Reo, Moon, Maxwell.

The Josenhans' car was the biggest and the best. It not only had ample room for six adults, but it had folding jump seats. This beautiful car was always filled with young adults and children being driven to Back River Methodist Church on Sundays. The Josenhans were good Lutherans, and they thought all children should go to Sunday school and church—any church but Mount Carmel, the Catholic Church. Father too was anti-Catholic (after all, hadn't Catholics burned Jan Hus at the stake?), but he had no objection to my going to a Protestant church with the Josenhans. And so I became a believer while Father remained a "free thinker." I practiced my storytelling by bringing home the Sunday school lessons and repeating them to my family who always listened. As a young adult, I had long political and philosophic discussions with Father, during which my excitement shed more heat than light. Our discussions always ended with my father saying, "Well, girl, I don't think either one of us is going to change the world." We had the mind stretching without the rancor, and we always ended as friends.

Sometime during the early 1920s, Uncle James and Aunt Marie and Cousin Charlie decided to return to Czechoslovakia. Aunt Marie suffered from frequent colds, and doctors thought the climate in Baltimore was too damp for her lungs. So they sold their shoemaking shop and went back to a more agreeable climate. At this time also, Father wanted to return. I do not remember the details except that by then I was in fourth grade and my teacher, Miss Langrall, always listened attentively as I told her all I knew of my family's plan to emigrate. Brother was excited too and began hoarding packs of all flavors of Wrigley's gum because he had heard there was *no* gum in that otherwise wonderful, beautiful country. Why we did not go, neither of us knows. Was there not enough money for passage? Couldn't we sell our place? Were not conditions as favorable there economically as they were here? Was either Father or Mother reluctant to give up what roots and goods they had established here?

Anyway, suddenly no one ever talked about going back, and we too entered the auto age with a half-ton Ford truck and also entered the poultry business full time. It was indeed a family business with all of us contributing to its success. It was 1924. Father was thirty-eight when he got his driver's license. I think I was his first passenger. Jerry remembers that the first Sunday after we got this little caged truck, our young, experienced driver-friend Jim Kozak took all the neighborhood children and young people for a ride. This sounds right; Father probably was brave enough to drive a load of chickens and one passenger, but not a load of giggling kids. But Jim, young and unafraid, enjoyed driving anyone's new vehicle filled with adoring and appreciative riders.

Our first truck with Mother at the wheel, 1924

As transportation changed from horse and wagon to cars, blacksmith shops slowly vanished, garages appeared, and roads were paved. Transitions were always children's delights, and sometimes headaches for adults. Eastern Avenue was redone with concrete shoulders and a macadam center. After the shoulders were poured, the surface became our after school skating ground and smooth runs for scooters and bikes. Ruthie Habicht even got a "girl's" bicycle and shared it with any girl who could ride. We all did. Jerry built his first car using wheels from the old express wagon. It had a working steering wheel, a hood with an alarm clock ticking like an engine, and even headlights—tin cans with short candles covered with wax paper. Of course, we had to push it, but it ran well on the new concrete and never lacked for pusher or driver. Then there was the kettle of tar, a slab of which was always fun to chew. What would this group think of next?

At home when our parents' occupation changed from tailoring to raising poultry, and we no longer removed swatches from cards of obsolete material, we spent many a winter night stripping duck and goose feathers. When ducks and geese were prepared for market, they were first dipped in hot water to make the feathers easier to pluck. Goose and duck down and some larger feathers we saved for down comforters, "featherbeds" we called them. The wet feathers were dried in large white muslin bags, and on winter evenings, we sat around the kitchen table and stripped away the feathers from the center quill. To keep these tiny feathers from flying all around the kitchen as we talked or laughed, we carefully pushed handfuls under a large mixing bowl placed upside down in the center of the table. Sometimes someone read aloud while the others stripped the dry feathers, and there were always refreshment breaks. Peeled and quartered apples and homemade chocolate fudge were still the favorites. Before long, many bags of stripped feathers were converted into featherbeds. Sometime later, the down from these simple covers was again emptied into bags, sent to Chicago, and stuffed into beautiful quilted comforters for my own and my brother's wedding beds. The large wing feathers, too coarse for bedding, were cleverly woven together to form pastry brushes, which we sold in the market. Nothing was wasted.

Father and Brother, 1922

Chapter VII:

Building the Poultry Business

Our first horse and wagon permitted us to explore back roads and visit friends with farms off the beaten path, but now with our new Ford truck, we really expanded our horizons. We were selling more chickens, ducks, geese, and turkeys than we could produce. Father branched out into buying poultry, not only locally, but also into Harford County, that lovely countryside with huge farms that grew corn, beans, and tomatoes, and raised beef and dairy cattle. Each Wednesday, Father and Brother left home at 5:00 AM and drove to Forest Hill, MD, and bought eggs, chickens, and other poultry from local farmers who brought them to the railroad station in town. Father always checked the morning paper to see what the wholesale price of these items was and paid the farmers the going rate. He was fair in his prices, always paying a little more for *fat* hens, which his Jewish customers prized. Chicken fat was a valued cooking product since our orthodox Jewish customers could not use lard as shortening.

Principal market days were Thursdays and Saturdays. Thursday was eggs, produce, and *live* poultry day. A good supply of fat stewing chickens always showed a good profit since the Jewish Sabbath meal was prepared on Friday. Saturday was *live* and dressed (without feathers) poultry day patronized mainly by the Christian population. Some of the older immigrant folks liked to kill their own chickens, sometimes buying several, and then fattening them up a little more since they liked that extra bit of chicken fat in their rich chicken noodle soup or in the gravy with a roasted chicken on Sunday. Soon the immigrants forgot their old country waste not, want not ways and preferred to buy their chickens dressed and cut up.

Father and Brother handled the "live" trade, and Mother and usually a woman helper handled the "dressed" sales. I was probably thirteen or fourteen before I was allowed to use the extra-sharp knife to split a frying chicken down the back—a feat that took skill and strength. The other special skill was separating the gall bladder from the liver; a sensitive, delicate procedure since you dared not break this sac and have the bitter green gall liquid flow on the liver. When a customer wanted the heart, liver, and gizzard, the cutting had to be meticulous, not *hulla bulla*. The customer gave the order and you did it right. The customer provided your livelihood; remember? Mother always waited on the critical customers and let me practice on the more forgiving or patient ones.

As Father traveled the countryside, he would often stop at orchards and buy bushels of fresh fruit. When he saw a cannery, he would pick up cases of freshly packed shoepeg corn (an excellent white sweet corn), and there were times when he would even get honey right out of a hive! In the market, we patronized fellow stall keepers who sold meats, imported fruits, pickles, fish, and cheeses. Snapshots of Mother now showed her less haggard, even pleasantly plump! Food was plentiful and good and varied, even exotic. I remember Father planting a purple potato used as a garnish in potato salad, and a large green-fleshed cantaloupe that was sweeter than the orange-fleshed ones. Some of these exotic foods worked out, others were unsalable, but the old standbys like tomatoes, string beans, and freshly cut sweet corn always sold.

The Matejkas in 1929 showing the results of prosperity

Another addition to our Saturday market business was changing our stall from selling poultry and eggs in the morning to selling "snowballs," crushed ice flavored with sweet syrup, in the afternoon. After people bought their regular weekend food, and cleaned their houses, many families went to the local movies, which often had vaudeville shows, sort of a double feature, on Saturdays. Then they would wander through the market looking for sweets. On hot summer days, snowballs were the favorite among the crowd. We offered many flavors, but chocolate topped the list. I remember Mother making a huge quantity of this chocolate flavored syrup, which had to be cooked and then kept refrigerated. Fruit flavors were easier to deal with. Mother cooked a sugar and water mixture, and then added a prepared fruit concentrate with each quart of sugar water. There were at least ten flavors: orange, lemon, grape, raspberry, strawberry, root beer, peach, custard, vanilla, and pineapple. All of these could be topped with marshmallow. We never used a hand shaver to create the ball of ice; as early as the twenties, we had an electric crusher that chopped ice finer than a manual shaver did and much faster. Father always believed in using a machine to do the heavy work. I remember our first chicken "plucker," a rotating drum with rubber fingers. Unfortunately, it did not pluck wing feathers or pinfeathers, which still had to be pulled out by hand, but it did save a lot of manual labor.

Many other changes occurred in the twenties. We sold two frontage lots to Leroy and Annie Hall and their daughter Bertha. They had a house on Ann Street, one block north of Eastern Avenue. They had a car and wanted to live on a paved road and on a streetcar line. Bertha was a year younger than I was. She was also born in October, so we became good friends almost immediately. After they sold their old house, they built a nice new one with a garage. This garage was the talk of the neighborhood. You could drive the car through the garage door and then drive it out again, still going forward! Mr. Hall was a stationary engineer for the B&O Railroad. It was his job to run the locomotive onto a turntable, check everything carefully, and then manually turn it around ready to head out again. He built a turntable in his garage so that he did not have to spoil his yard with a big driveway to turn around in.

The Halls fenced their property and planted beautiful roses along the fence. Or did we fence in our property along their property line? In those days if you had a place of business and had a dog, you had to keep the dog chained. Our dog was chained to his doghouse, but at night, we locked the front gate and let him run loose. So perhaps it was our fence between our property and the Halls' because they did not have an outdoor dog, and they were not in business.

Anyway, Bertha was probably in grade five or six, and I was a year ahead. She and I both had scooters during the time that Brother and Ruthie Habicht had bikes. During the winter, on Saturdays, when my parents thought it was too cold for me to stay inside the unheated market all day, Bertha would spend the day with me at home. My job was to give our hired man lunch if he was on duty that weekend and to be sure that Bertha had as many eggs as she could eat. She loved fried eggs sunny-side up and delighted in filling a frying pan with four or five eggs. She would systematically eat the soft centers with a piece of bread and then make sandwiches of the whites. My favorite meal was a can of Mitchell's Shoepeg Corn. We thought these lunches were wonderful! The hired man ate a large plate of thick barley soup and what always seemed like a whole pound of hot dogs with a half loaf of bread! I can still hear the natural casing of the hot dog crunch when he bit into it with one of his few teeth. It was simple food, but plenty of it. We all liked this variety—something for everyone. After lunch, Bertha and I straightened the house a bit, played the old pump organ, and sang hymns.

The neighborhood in 1933 from our backyard

There were other big changes. Our section of Eastern Avenue road became "Metropolitan," so the tax bill stated. We got electricity! No more wicks to trim, chimneys to clean, and flashlights to keep at bedside. But we country folk knew electricity cost money and did not turn on lights before dark, or leave lights burning in unoccupied rooms. Our neighbors, the Lauensteins, one long country block away, used to say their mother would not let them turn their lights on until the Matejkas turned on theirs. There were no houses between the two families then. Nightfall was a ritual; someone went around our house, closed all the shutters while someone inside hooked the shutters tight, and someone else locked the gate and unchained the dog.

There were seasonal rituals as well. During summer, light (white) shades were replaced with dark blue ones, wool rugs were changed to oval grass ones, and screens were put in. Then in late fall, lace curtains were washed, starched, put on stretchers, and put on windows, which now had white shades again. The ritual to darken the house was for comfort and appearance, and in case Brother had another attack of measles. Dr. Mace, who made house calls, always told Mother to keep Jerry's room dark for a week or more as a precaution against blindness. I know I had measles only once, but Jerry had one kind or another at least four times.

And then city water from the reservoir at Loch Raven, purified at Montebello, came our way. Our kitchen sported a sink (which we pronounced "zinc") instead of a bucket of drinking water with a dipper, and a bathroom appeared on the now closed-in back porch. I remember our school "companions" or pencil boxes that held our pencils, pens, pen points, et cetera, and always had a folding cup that never seemed to last a whole year. The school had a pump, and we would say to someone, "Pump for me." If you did not have a cup, you would cup your hands, get a quick drink of cold water, and incidentally wash your grubby hands—primitive but doable. No one was denied a drink of water with or without a cup.

Living in a metropolitan district also meant families had to give up so many feet of road frontage for future improvements such as road widening and sewage disposal. So we fenced in our property, but we also had to cut the grass on the "metro" side. We used a push mower with a rotary blade to cut the grass. We were glad the grass in the orchard did not need cutting every week, as did the other areas. Mother kept her flower gardens cultivated, and Brother and the hired man did the larger areas. Summer was a busy time because we were in business full time. Everyone had chores to do daily, even on Sundays.

Sometime during the twenties, our church, Back River Methodist, burned. It had been a wooden structure, and one Saturday night the furnace overheated and the building burned to the ground by Sunday morning. The Josenhans offered the use of their hall for church services while a new concrete black structure (no more wooden buildings) was under construction. The Sunday school children sold "blocks" for twenty-five cents each to help rebuild the church, and the child who sold the most blocks received special recognition. The winner was the child of a summer visitor who was a postmaster in an affluent northern suburb whose patrons gladly bought a block or two or four to rebuild the poor little country church whose poor little waifs had no place to learn about God and Jesus. To them we were a mission church and they were our missionary angels. The interim church was great for the five Lauenstein kids and me. We could now walk to Sunday school. I remember one of the "Chicken Patty" dinners held in the Josenhans' Rossville academy hall. Mother took my brother and me, but made sure she fed us a hardy snack before we left so we would not act as if we had not eaten for a week. She need not have worried; we were both too shy among adults even to dream of asking for second helpings.

Essex School changed from six to seven to eight grades. Small country schools like neighboring Back River had only six grades and then, providing their own transportation, students could go on to larger schools like ours four or five miles away for seventh and eighth grades. Finally, students could go to a regional high school through grade eleven. In our area, seventh and eighth graders went by streetcar (#23 transferring to #26) to Sparrows Point for occasional shop and home economics classes. Some kids were excused from these courses because they became "car sick" on the streetcar. Jerry enjoyed going to school; making something out of wood in a shop was a nice break from history and geography. He also enjoyed the countywide track and field meets held annually at Patterson Park in Baltimore City. Mothers would pack picnic lunches, and whole families would watch their young athletes compete.

If I remember correctly, there were five high schools in the county during the twenties: Catonsville and Towson (the large academic high schools), Franklin and Sparks (the schools in the farming areas), and Sparrows Point (the industrial school). The towns of Essex, Middle River, and Chase did not qualify for high schools, so those students, who wanted to, could either go by train to Baltimore or transfer to Towson, or they could go to Sparrows Point by streetcar. Both routes were circuitous and time consuming. When Glen L. Martin built his aircraft factory in Middle River in 1928, many sixteen-year-old eighth graders worked at the factory and continued their education at night at the Maryland

Institute, which taught drafting, blue printing, and industrial design. Father wanted Jerry to go to this evening school while joining him in his prospering poultry business, but Jerry had had enough of school and was content to do more interesting things like drive the half-ton truck over back country roads at age fourteen. When he was sixteen, he had no trouble going to Bel Air to get his driver's license. After all, he had two years of driving experience.

Meanwhile I continued to go to the newly built large Essex School where seventh graders changed classes and had a different teacher for math, language, history, and geography. Then as eighth graders, we took math, science, civics, Latin, and English, had our own library room and played basketball in one of the empty portables. Walking home was more interesting then because there were new kids from the outlying areas to walk with. We were older and began to talk about adult happenings like Lindbergh's nonstop flight to Paris (1927) and tales of bootleg whiskey being locally distilled in secluded waterfront places.

Two important things happened in my life during the summer of 1928. Toward the end of the school year when elementary teachers had meetings, the principal asked two of us eighth graders to teach two first grade classes for a day. Ever since fourth grade, I had been saying I wanted to be a teacher when I grew up. So Bill Peters and I became teachers for a day. It was a long day and harder than I expected, but one week after school was out, we each received a check from the board of education. I have forgotten how much it was (two dollars maybe), but I was in heaven! A bit later that summer, we eighth grade graduates received notification by postcard that a bus would begin running from our area to Sparrows Point High School. Cost was a dollar a week. Could I go? Would my parents pay my bus fare? Were any of my new friends going? Yes, many of us would go, starting at Chase, stopping at Bengies, Middle River, along Eastern Avenue, Mace Avenue, and North Point Road—a fourteen-mile trip. Our horizons were expanding, and I began my dream of becoming a teacher.

Matejka's Quality Poultry Farm, 1938
Left to right: unidentified friend, Jerry, Father, Cousin Charlie, his wife
Lillian, and Mother

Chapter VIII:

How We Survived the Great Depression

Father's decision to go into the poultry business paid off. Within two years, the small half-ton Ford Model T truck was traded in for a one-ton model and by 1928, a new Model A open body truck was added. For local, shorter trips, the smaller truck was used, and during holidays both trucks were out bringing home so many chickens, ducks, geese, and turkeys that a new big barn was built. It was a well-designed building—two stories high and larger than our house. On the right was a feed storage room, truck high, so that a truck bringing one hundred pound bags of feed backed up to the feed-room platform and the bags were easily slid from truck to platform to room without lifting. On the right side was the poultry-dressing room with water heater, picking table, and new automatic chicken "plucker."

The middle-front section was the truck entry with two large barn doors, one of which had a small door for personal entrance. Behind these three sections was a large, long room with windows across the back and right side filled with "batteries" or wire chicken cages on rollers. Two tiers high, there were four sections per tier, each section holding four to six chickens depending on the size of the birds. Feed troughs and water containers served each section and metal trays caught the droppings.

I can still see the big truck pulling into the middle section to put a load of chickens in the wooden-dowelled coops under shelter while Father and Brother came into the house for a hot meal, which Mother had ready for them. After their meal, Father and Brother and usually a hired man, transferred the chickens into the metal batteries in the sunlit back room, and fed and watered the hens. This was on Wednesdays. On Thursdays, Mother, Father, and Brother took a load of eggs, produce, and live chickens to the market, and I went to school.

Thursday was only a half market day, so when I came home from school, everyone was home resting and preparing for a busy day on Friday, which was poultry "dressing" day. A section of that large back room in the barn was the place where Father killed the chickens with a special instrument, which left no visible wound. We weighed and sold the "dressed" chickens with heads and feet intact. At the customer's request, the hens were "cleaned," heads and feet cut off, and entrails removed. On Fridays, Father killed the chickens, Mother dipped them in hot water, Brother used the plucking machine, and everyone finished picking off the feathers the machine skipped. Then we cooled the chickens in tubs of cold water and iced them in metal cans.

Ducks were prepared the same way, but in smaller quantities or by ordering ahead. They were harder to dress. Their oily feathers did not yield to the rubber fingers of the plucking machine and so had to be hand-plucked. We raised most of our own Muscovy ducks. Father very carefully kept white feathered drakes and ducks to avoid black pinfeathers as on black-and-white ducks. Our customers preferred Muscovy ducks to Long Island ducks because they were less fatty and had all dark meat.

In the summer, we added all kinds of fresh produce to our poultry selection. I remember how incredibly long Fridays were. After plucking feathers until three or four in the afternoon and cleaning all the work surfaces, we bunched "soup herbs." Father would pick a basket of parsley, celery, and carrots from the garden, and then Mother and I would make little bouquets of parsley and celery, add a carrot, tie the posy, carefully trim the stems, and breathe a sigh of relief when we reached the bottom of the basket. Those little bouquets, so prized for chicken soup, sold for two cents each. While we were bunching soup herbs, Brother would cut several burlap bags of sweet corn and pick a basket or two of tomatoes. Corn had to be "fresh cut," so that was always the last chore on Friday evening. With a new tractor added to our farm equipment, our gardens kept getting bigger and bigger.

Fortunately, our customers appreciated produce fresh from the farm, and I am sure these little additions paid my school bus fare and our little luxuries like Czech records, weekly jigsaw puzzles, and magazines. I especially remember the *Saturday Evening Post* whose Norman Rockwell covers Jerry and I pasted on one wall of the truck entrance of the barn.

Ah yes, and the barn had a huge second floor where seasonal things like porch chairs and rockers and extra large turkey and goose coops were stored. There was always a very wide center aisle where you could practice dance steps all by yourself. It was sometime during the early thirties when we got our first car (a maroon

Model A Ford town sedan) that a group of us went to Fink's Dancing School to learn the two-step, fox trot, waltz, et cetera. I remember stealing away to the barn attic to practice the dance steps between lessons. Nothing came easily to me; I always had to work hard at everything, but I practiced and improved.

Mother and me, 1930

While my parents' poultry business thrived, I was having new learning experiences—academic, social, and practical. The fourteen-mile trip to Sparrows Point High School was an adventure. We were a busload, thirty or so students in all stages of adolescent development. Some very tall, some tiny, some maturely dressed and groomed, some ready for adult responsibility, some childish, some born leaders. We all had two things in common: our parents could afford to pay our bus fare, and we were willing to go to school. We did all kinds of things on those long trips to and from high school. We sang all the popular songs with Ruth Collison standing in the bus step-well leading us. Or, we matched pennies, especially with Pauline whose parents owned a grocery store. Her penny stack always had a sprinkling of "Indian Heads," which were prized as collector's items. Sometimes we read our history assignment or studied Latin verbs. The return trip was less exuberant. We had full schedules (Latin I, English II, history, geometry, home ec/shop, and phys ed). The school had no cafeteria, so we carried our lunches or went to the village sweet shop for a ten-cent sandwich, and a five-cent Coke or a ten-cent milkshake. By 3:30 PM we were tired, hungry, and ready to go home; but once home, we could not wait to call a friend we had just left to ask about an assignment or finish a bit of news we thought of after we had had something to eat. Our peers were now our friends, family, and advisors.

My best friend since junior high school, Marie Elton Plummer, on our
bicycling trip through the Smoky Mountains, 1930

By grade ten, our junior year in high school, we had to decide which course we would take—general, commercial, or academic. Sixteen credits were required for graduation, but four had to be in English, one in American history, one in math, one in science, and the rest depending on which course you had selected. Sparrows Point had excellent shop courses in both wood and metal. We were proud of our woodshop boys. Desks they had made were on exhibit at the Maryland State Fair in Timonium. We also had good soccer and lacrosse teams. I remember one boy who always came to play soccer in September, and then he dropped out and returned in the spring to play lacrosse. He took regular courses too, but he never finished his studies so did not graduate. Well liked by students and faculty, he was always welcomed back. In the twenties and early thirties, schools were available for anyone to attend—up to age twenty.

Probably the hardest course in our school was the commercial course. Students had to have a grade C or better in both English and math, and strict standards were set for both speed and accuracy. The academic course required two years of Latin and French, in addition to the regular curriculum. By tenth grade, students from our area and Sparrows Point and Dundalk were well integrated in classes and extracurricular activities.

In spite of our adolescent exuberance and bravado, a note of sadness frequently ran through our group. Eva's father died in an accident at Bethlehem Steel. She was the eldest of a large family. We learned to write notes of condolence in English class and to express our concern by helping where and how we could. There was no company insurance, no welfare system. Eva finished her junior year, but did not return. This was reality. Maturity was sometimes imposed sooner than expected. Signs of the aftermath of the 1929 stock market crash also began surfacing. The student fare on the bus from Edgemere to Sparrows Point High School was five cents, but eight cents bought a loaf of bread, and out of work parents had to make difficult choices. There was no unemployment check to tide people over. Perhaps that fifteen-year-old junior could help by running errands for tips or, in some cases, hop a freight train and "go west," making one less mouth to feed at home.

Our English teacher, Miss Krug, was very helpful in teaching us written expression like "readable" letters of application and being grammatically correct when speaking. "It isn't enough to have on clean clothes and polished shoes when you go for an interview," she would say. "But as a high school graduate, you should have the potential to represent the company by being able to think clearly and speak grammatically." No ain'ts, youse, we was, or him and me can do it, she would preach. "It hurts my ears," she would say with half a grin when someone lapsed into Sparrows Point street language, and she would make the offender say it over correctly. But we could see how sad she was when she had to sign someone's school withdrawal slip. "Are you sure you want to quit just because you're sixteen today? Can't you finish out this year and graduate?" she would say to a good student being pressured by his family to go out and get a job. Usually the student had to quit because family pressure was too much, but these events strengthened the rest of us in our resolve to finish what we started. We were eventually convinced that an education was desirable and important.

By the end of my junior year, I wanted to go to college, and not just the State Normal School (Teacher's College) at Towson, which by then had changed from a two-year training school to three years. I wanted to go to Goucher, the college Miss Krug attended. After all, it was only one year longer than Normal School, and when I graduated, I was eligible to teach high school level. And so, in my senior year, I took all the proper courses needed for admission: English IV, French II, physics, American history, solid geometry, and trig, and audited Latin II. Goucher required learning a classical language as well as a modern language. By then I knew I did not want to continue French and my Latin was rusty, so I filled my schedule fuller than full, just in case my parents sent me to a *good* private school. I could dream, couldn't I?

Mother and me when I graduated from college in 1935

Chapter IX:

A College Girl

Step by step the dream comes first, then the planning, then the work. If you are lucky, have good family support, and make appropriate changes as you go along; you have a good chance of being successful. Father said he did not like school himself, but if I really wanted to become a teacher, he would pay my way. Wow! I would go to Goucher! My high school teachers were so proud. My first year Latin teacher said she hoped to induct me into her chapter of Phi Beta Kappa; my physics teacher wrote in my autograph book, "Great accomplishments are expected of you, you are capable of them." And Miss Krug had a tea for me that summer to wish me well.

But I was a shy, sixteen-year-old country girl with much to learn, so my first semester was a real struggle. College classes were six days a week and taught at double speed. Nothing was repeated as in high school. A normal load was five subjects, each three times a week. What I did not realize was that the professor's lecture covered only about one-third of the material you were expected to master; the rest was outside reading, lab work, and research. At first I made the mistake of thinking that if I did not have a scheduled class I could go downtown (Goucher was in the city in those days) to see a matinee or even a double feature. Needless to say, I soon learned that unscheduled afternoons were to be spent in libraries or labs, or on the college hockey field.

And though Father promised to pay my way, I'm sure he must have had second thoughts several times those four years, especially when his friends said, "You're sending a *girl* to school? She'll just get married." And then Father thought Jerry deserved more money, but he didn't feel he could afford my tuition and a raise for Jerry, so I made a bargain with Father: send me to school and give Jerry a piece of property. And this we did. In 1936, when Jerry was considering marriage, Father gave him a lot on which to build his house.

We were so lucky we felt covered with horseshoes! In March 1933, President Roosevelt declared a "bank holiday" that forced the closure of the nation's banks and halted all financial transactions for five days to determine which banks were insolvent. As I remember it, Father had withdrawn money to buy chickens on Wednesday, just before the banks closed on Thursday.

So with a week's supply of chickens bought and paid for, Father continued his business without interruption. Of course, the bank closure froze the money in my parents' personal account. Later those funds were repaid at a very small percentage of their worth, but the loss was minimal compared to what so many others had lost. Many of my fellow Goucher students were forced to withdraw from school, and their younger brothers and sisters could not go to college at all. This was a sad time for investors. Many could not recover their huge losses and chose to end their lives.

Brother in front of the newly stuccoed house, 1934

We were lucky about not only the timing of the "bank holiday," but we had just made and paid for big improvements to the business—the new, efficient barn, a four-car garage, the stuccoed house, and the grounds landscaped. Father proudly displayed a National Recovery Act (NRA) sticker, hired extra help, and was positive he and President Roosevelt would bring prosperity back to the nation. In 1933, the federal minimum wage was twenty-five cents per hour. If each small businessman could hire *one* extra man, we'd be on our way to recovery. While businessmen did their share, the government sent unemployed young people to civilian conservation corps camps, and older unemployed persons to the works progress administration to build roads and parks. The problem, however, was bigger than both my father and President Roosevelt had anticipated. Graduates complained that it was not what you knew, but whom you knew. World War I veterans marched in Washington for bonuses, and workers complained that sixteen dollars a week was not enough to pay the rent and feed their families.

But through it all, ordinary people were very creative. Owners of seashore places charged their guests a twenty-five cent shore fee, and groups of city folk packed lunches and spent a hot summer Sunday at the seashore. Real estate was turning over rapidly, and Father arranged a sale of a forty-acre farm with waterfront on Seneca Creek to a Czech farmer from Nebraska. In spite of the farmer's hard work and some help from us, he became anxious about not being able to meet mortgage payments; so Father resold the place to our old friends, the Nenadals from Curtis Bay, who wanted to retire from their dry goods store. Besides having a quiet waterfront spot, they put up a mushroom shed and grew a fine crop of snow-white mushrooms to sell to restaurants. The Justls went back to Nebraska and corresponded with us for many years.

During this period, Father made a sand bowling alley in the pinewoods on the "back four acres" where older folks spent many a Sunday afternoon bowling ten pins. During those nippy fall days, they would roast oysters, have an eighth of beer, and sing their old drinking songs. Father thought that the pinewoods enclave would be great for serving duck dinners, but Mother squelched that idea. She was willing to sell dressed ducks on Saturday, but she did not want to cook them for the public on Sundays.

The younger folks did not want to stay around with the "old" folks, so we piled into a car and went for a nice long drive. I remember once a cop stopped us for exceeding the speed limit in a small Pennsylvania town and took us to the local police station to pay the fine. I do not remember how much the fine was (five dollars maybe), but we did not have that much among the four of us. So I offered to put up my black onyx high school ring as collateral. I think the officers settled for what money we had without the ring. We were glad to get back and have refreshments with the "old" folks.

There was good camaraderie among the young people of our church. We borrowed family assets for our parties. Aunt Helen's place next to Cape May Beach for watermelon parties, Aunt Gertie's clubroom for Saturday night dances, our sand bowling alley lighted with Japanese lanterns for night bowling, and the church basement for deck tennis. Everybody's aunt was *our* aunt, and everybody's house was a good place for simple refreshments. We ice-skated on the gravel pit pond and held play rehearsals at Mrs. Holzknecht's lovely home. We never needed much money. We knew how to make our own entertainment and share what we had. Father did not allow me to date while attending college, so these group activities were nice social outlets. Since jobs for young people were hard to get, many couples delayed marriage. When they heard, "Oh, go ahead and get married, two can live as cheaply as one," they replied, "Yes, but only half as long!"

After four years of hard work, I graduated from Goucher College with a major in mathematics and a minor in history and German and joined the ranks of job hunters. I checked in with investment bankers on Redwood Street and stopped at Equitable Bank whose manager was Mr. Hunzlik of Czech extraction. Father thought it might be helpful to tell him I too was Czech. Not so. Mr. Hunzlik did not care about my ethnic origin. He said, "Can you type? The trouble with you girls is that you graduate from college and can't do anything. Go take a business [secretarial] course." Well, no way was I going to type! But I did get a job. I hand addressed envelopes on a rickety table under dim lights on the night shift and received two dollars per thousand. I did about a thousand a night and made a total of $10.50. I proudly gave my mother five dollars for room and board, paid five dollars carfare, and came out with fifty cents for myself—this, after four years of high tuition study.

After that, I sent applications for a math teaching position to the twenty-three counties in Maryland. Several public institutions responded. Some private boarding schools offered forty dollars a month, plus room and board if I had interest in being a dorm mother and a teacher. Yikes! Finally, I received a call from C.G. Cooper, superintendent of Baltimore County schools offering a job to teach math and science at either Catonsville or Towson. Angels were sitting on both my shoulders! I became a teacher at Towson High School. The amazing part was that the year before, the teachers had taken a voluntary pay cut (because the county was short of money from so many delinquent tax bills), but this year the cut was not to be reinstated, so I would start at full pay. Of course, I would be on substitute's pay until my supervisor okayed my work, a test period of two to three months. Wow, was I lucky making two hundred dollars a month when minimum wage was twenty-five cents per hour.

Of course, I worked more than forty hours a week. I taught during the day and planned the next day's classes at night. Since I had no car, I had to take the

#23 streetcar to Fayette and Calvert, then transfer to the #8 to Towson, and then walk five blocks to the school on Central Avenue—more than an hour each way. I decided to get a room in Towson and go home on weekends, a very smart move. Except for one uncooperative class, all my classes were good, and the science department faculty was very helpful. Students needing financial help to stay in school were hired by the science department to help make demonstration models. These models were a big help in teaching and took a lot of time to make, so it was wonderful to have these models already made. I became a certified teacher in two months. I lived with Mrs. Moncure, our school librarian until spring, and then I bought my first brand new car—thanks to my father's lessons in saving accounts. With my new car and job, I was in heaven and promptly moved back home.

But heaven lasted only a week or two after my first year of teaching. During June 1936, Father went into the hospital. He had been having urinary problems, and his urologist suggested he go through a series of tests at the University of Maryland Hospital. I went to see him in his private room at the hospital, and he appeared in good spirits. He did not seem concerned about the expenses because he believed he could pay the bill very easily by buying more chickens, raising more turkeys, or selling another piece of property. When I left his room, the urologist told me the news—cancer of the bladder—six months to live. Not *my* father, not the immigrant who sent me through college, gave Jerry a piece of land for his house, and the proud owner of a business! Well, the doctors gave him a series of x-ray treatments and then put him on morphine to deaden the pain, but the cancer was rampant! Why me, Lord? I was only twenty-one, too young for this kind of news. How could I tell my mother and conceal it from Father? As it turned out, Father lived for seven more years, but those years were a blur to all of us. We buried ourselves in our work and activities.

Brother's wife Lottie with their older daughter, Rosalie, in front of the
new house, ca. 1945

Jerry built his house and married Lottie Vanik in 1937. I drove my little green car to Towson and back, a twenty-two minute drive. I enjoyed teaching and liked my colleagues; I was active in the church, dated a Czech dentist, and went out as often as I could to make up for the college years when Father allowed only study and work.

Father seemed better, still doing his share of the work, but not with his usual enthusiasm. Could the doctors be wrong? A whole year had passed. I decided to go to summer school that summer (1937) to get credits to renew my teaching certificate and start work on my masters. Most of our faculty went to Columbia, but Helen Hale and I attended Cornell—driving together in my little green car.

Father and I decided to go to Europe to visit his birthplace. He had waited a long time for this opportunity, and now he was going with his teacher-daughter. He would be a gracious and attentive escort and host, and Mother and Brother would take care of his business. Unfortunately, like the earlier planned trips, this was not to be. In 1938, Germany invaded Poland. Traveling to Czechoslovakia was out of the question. Meanwhile, Uncle James, who had returned to the homeland in 1924, foresaw the German threat and encouraged his son Charles and Charles's friendly and loveable wife Lillian to return to the United States where Charles had been born. I had sent Charles his American birth certificate, and in return, they brought a tiny tin of Czech soil to my homesick father.

The young couple occupied a room in Jerry and Lottie's new house, but ate meals at our house just next door. Lillian was surprised that I, a teacher, helped Mother wash dishes after dinner. Sorry, Lil, no class privileges allowed in democratic America! And Father kept on living and helping people in spite of his poor health. Lillian still talks about Father lending her and Charles money for a down payment on their house, since the conflict in Europe disallowed them from taking money from out of their country. And she always emphasizes, "He lent us money without a promissory note and without interest. What a great guy he was!" Yes, many people remember Father that way.

Father

My husband, Jack, in uniform at our house on Sue Creek, ca. 1943

Chapter X:

The Forties

War and illness are a bad combination. Fortunes are made and lost, people are shifted about voluntarily and involuntarily; and if you cannot move with the flow, you are hopelessly helpless. In spite of our country's desire to remain out of Europe's war, the temptation to produce war material was too great. Factories began hiring more people so again there was a population shift. This time folks from West Virginia, Pennsylvania, and Ohio would be more careful with their money. They would pay off their home mortgages and after the war could retire to their own home free of debt, or so they thought. The Martin plant in Middle River was a big drawing card that hired a lot of new people and put them to work in three shifts. New apartments went up quickly, trailers arrived in town, and people rented spare rooms in their homes. Unfortunately, we could not deliver war materials safely to countries at war without getting involved in World War II, the war to end all wars.

How did preparation for, and involvement in, World War II affect the Matej-kas? It surely was not easy on Father and Mother. Father slowly deteriorated and was in constant pain, alleviated only temporarily with strong and stronger doses of morphine. Most friends stopped coming because visiting was not fun any-more, live-in hired help needed more supervision and service than Mother could provide, and Jerry and Lottie had a new baby—Rosalie, born in 1939. I had a new boyfriend, a non-Czech displaced from Cleveland, Ohio, by way of Virginia, whose family was eking out a living until "things got better" in the cities. Jack was a fun person, active in the Mountain Club, and trying his hand in advertis-ing. With a full teaching schedule and working with a Junior Boys Club in church, I was not home much.

Father and I still had philosophic discussions occasionally, mainly about Tomáš Masaryk's presidency of Czechoslovakia and bits and pieces of trivia. I still had a pretty good understanding of Czech and even tried to learn Czech grammar by enrolling for a year or two in an evening class. But to carry on a lengthy, meaningful conversation in half English and half Czech was a real struggle. Father appreciated the effort and I enjoyed the challenge. Mother's real concern was Father's heavy smoking. He frequently fell asleep at the kitchen table late at night with a lighted cigarette burning blisters on his fingers before the pain awakened him. Poor Mother, toward the end she hardly slept at all. And I remember Father's saying to me, "If I'm ever poor, don't bring me food, bring me cigarettes and lady fingers." And this I was able to do.

Jack and I were married on January 1, 1941, taking advantage of my two-week Christmas break. It was a small home wedding—just our families and a few friends. Marie Elton, my good friend from high school days was my maid of honor, and Arthur Heise, Jack's friend, was best man. Lillian helped mother with refreshments, Jerry took movies of the occasion, and everyone waved us off for a brief skiing honeymoon in New Germany, Maryland. Some of our friends thought we should have had a big church wedding, and business friends thought we should have had a big reception in the Sokol hall. But I thought Father and Mother were getting too exhausted for this type of excitement and that a small family wedding was more appropriate.

Ethel Ebersberger from the Young People's church group had a quick wedding shower for me when she saw my Christmas diamond and learned of our plans for a home wedding. The faculty of Towson High School had a surprise "snow" shower later, after a spy reported what was lacking in our apartment on 217 West Lanvale Street. That was some apartment! It was the top (third) floor of the home of Henry Berge, a local sculptor who had his studio on the first floor and rented the other two floors (four apartments) to eke out a living and pay his mortgage. Our apartment had a large bedroom, bath, kitchen, dining alcove, large living room with a working fireplace, and a den—and even a garage for my 1939 black Chevrolet sedan.

The rent was forty dollars a month, but do not tell Mother and Father. They will think it is ridiculous to pay that much. Why you could buy a house and your mortgage payment would not be that much. True! Besides, it is too big, too much for Slava to care for while she is working. But we had answers for everything and listened to nobody. Jack and I had super glorious, one and a half years in that charming apartment. We even had a cleaning woman come in a half day a week. She cleaned and did my personal laundry. How beautiful those taffeta slips were when they were ironed damp-dry! We invited everyone to visit and showed off the rooms by having groups of four play a card game of hearts in each room. High scorers moved on to the next room—a type of musical chairs/hearts game.

We had simple desserts and popped corn and toasted marshmallows in the fire-place. Life was great except for a few annoyances.

A letter from the country superintendent of schools stated, "You should have told us you were being married. It is our policy not to keep married women on our staff unless their work is superior." Wow! Superior? Was my work superior? Women could vote now, but their work had to be superior to men's in order to keep a job. I need not have worried! In September of 1940, Congress approved the country's first peacetime draft, and already men were being drafted. Some protested, saying "Let God save the Queen this time," while others were so furious with Hitler that they enlisted or took their ire out on anyone with a German name. Hausner's Restaurant had its windows broken several times.

Father listened to his shortwave radio and thought that Hitler's masterful voice and constant repetition of Germany as the Master race had all blond, blue-eyed Germans convinced they were invincible. Then there was Mussolini just as convincing, just as power mad, and the Japanese seeking to be the principal rulers over all. Were not they also a superior race enjoying their victories? And here we were sending tons of scrap iron to Japan and first aid supplies to China. What was happening to our world and the worth of the individual and fellowship of man? If only bloodthirsty tyrants would fight each other and let the rest of us live in peace—even if we had to work very hard to have a little place of our own and share what we did have. But life was not always that simple.

On December 7, 1941, only eleven months after we were married, Japan's air-planes dropped bombs on our ships anchored at Pearl Harbor, and President Roosevelt asked Congress to declare war. Germany and Italy promptly declared war on the United States.

Immediately our personal world changed. What choices did we have? Wars were no longer one man shooting or bayoneting another, but airplanes and bombing raids sending people to air raid shelters, and submarines blowing up ships carrying soldiers and supplies. Destruction everywhere! Would our country be next? Was anyone, anywhere, safe anymore?

I cannot remember the day-by-day, hour-by-hour thoughts and emotions we experienced that month of December 1941, but suddenly my high school stu-dents were grown men and women instead of the carefree adolescents of only a month ago. Some enlisted immediately and others waited for the draft, stalling for "live" time, saying, "I'd rather be a live coward than a dead hero." Others, more calmly, went to school, plowed their family's fields at night, and freeing their fathers and older brothers to work in defense plants like Bendix, Black and

Decker, Martins, et cetera. Other students continued their education toward graduation and did all kinds of humanitarian volunteer work.

Jack and I, reeling from new and heavier responsibilities, took a brief, after-Christmas skiing trip to Mount Washington, New Hampshire, and stopped to visit with Aunt Isobel and Uncle Orville in Massachusetts. Aunt Isobel, Jack's father's sister, was a charming, gracious hostess who could make you feel most welcome even if you arrived very late at night with three extra people. I had always wanted to be that kind of hostess, but must admit I always fell short of her excellence.

Sue Creek in front of our house, ca. 1943

The Matejkas experienced many changes in 1942. Mother suddenly got very tired of all the work and responsibility of the poultry trade and caring for Father. She gave up the business. Brother sold his house and moved from the area. Jack's mother and father, who had bought a waterfront place on Sue Creek and divided the house into two apartments, wanted to sell, and Jack and I persuaded our friends Marie and Clary Plummer to buy it jointly with us, since neither of us could swing the mortgage alone. Jack's father had divided the property into three sections hoping to make a profit and buy a small farm. I remember Father, tired and ill, saying to Fred, "You don't want a farm. Farms are for the young." And

Father's saying to us, "Why don't you buy all three pieces. You don't have the money anyway so you may as well borrow for the whole tract." As I mentioned earlier, we heard what was being said, but would do it *our* way. How wonderful it was to be able to do some things your own way, even if they did not turn out exactly as you had planned or you recognize too late the wisdom of "older folks."

Some things you had no control over. Just two weeks after buying the house, Jack received his draft notice and had only two weeks to report for duty. We took a quick bicycle trip with the American Youth Hostels group, our last freely chosen vacation, gave up the big apartment, and rented the small efficiency one behind the large one, which was rented to my teaching friends from Maine, Ella Glines, and Velma Brown. So we still had our own apartment—small but private, and having colleagues in the same house turned out to be a comfort to me with Jack now serving in the Army Air Corps for the "duration."

Ration books appeared in 1942 allotting gasoline, heating oil, sugar, meat, and shoes. Rubber products including tires became scarce; inner tubes had patches upon patches. We learned to use a car jack, lug nut wrench, and tire iron, and to apply a patch to the inner tube.

Lucky people had a spare tire. They changed the tire and dropped off the flat at a filling station, hoping not to have another flat on the way to work. Five of us carpooled in two cars. I left my car in my parents' garage, and every other week, when it was my turn to drive, I rode the streetcar to pick it up.

Teachers handed out ration books, and people received the coupons for gasoline according to their occupation. Those working in defense plants received the most because they were vital to the war effort. Teachers received much less being *not* vital to the war effort. The number of persons living in the house determined heating oil. Folks not wishing to rent out rooms were often cold. If they had fireplaces, they burned wood or coal or rolled newspaper to raise the house temperature a few degrees. Mother and Father had a big coal-burning stove in their living room that heated the downstairs very well. But our house on Sue Creek had hot water oil heat and the radiators were frequently lukewarm. There were all kinds of stories about the hardships experienced and ingenious solutions. For example, a doctor making a house call came out to find his car jacked up and his tires stolen. A note left on the car windshield read, "Sorry, Doc, you can get them. We can't." With many doctors needed in the services and few allowed to go to school, civilian doctors requested that patients come to the office. There was some exchange of coupons for Post Exchange (PX) items like sugar and stamps for cigarettes and other items sold on the black market. One enterprising salesman appeared at the back door of a general store in Texas offering to sell a truckload of sugar in brown bags (two pounds in each bag) without sugar stamps. There was never enough sugar, so the storekeeper bought it readily, but soon customers returned the packages; the brown bags contained white sand.

Our friends, the Young People's group at the house on Sue Creek, ca. 1943

Jack spent his early military processing and training in Petersburg, Virginia, hitchhiking home whenever he could get a pass, so we were glad to have our own apartment and shore place. I remember one weekend when the upstairs shore tenants, a couple from Ithaca, treated us to a Sunday dinner. Mickey and Tracey had caught about thirty sun perch, filleted them (this was a day's work!) and prepared a special treat in honor of a soldier home on leave for a few hours. And folks driving always picked up soldiers in uniform. There were even small shelters along main highways for soldiers waiting for rides back to camp.

Soon summer was over. I went back to teaching, and Jack received orders to Champaign, Illinois, for training as a weatherman. He could not come home for Christmas, so I planned to spend my Christmas vacation near his camp. Father pressed a twenty-dollar bill in my hand (a lot of money when I was making forty-eight dollars a month) and said, "Go out for a nice dinner on Christmas Eve. You'll both be homesick." Jack and I met in Chicago where the hotel manager gave us a lovely room at discount rates (because he wanted us to come back after the war), and we went to an expensive restaurant for dinner and spent Father's gift. Father was right; we were homesick, but glad to be together in a nice place.

Meantime, Jerry joined the Merchant Marines. He got his training at Sheepshead Bay, NY. Jerry crossed the Atlantic many times assigned to the engine room, had several near misses, and was always glad to take as much leave as he could when his ship docked in Baltimore. In June 1943, Jerry went to the Marine Hospital in Baltimore for a hernia operation.

Shaw Field in Texas was Jack's next assignment. Father's health had been failing rapidly. Jack was not close by, and I really wanted to spend summer vacation with him since his assignment permitted him to live off base. Not knowing how much longer Father would live, this being seven years after the urologist's prediction of six months, I visited Jerry in the hospital in nearby Baltimore and said I would really like to spend the summer with Jack. I told Jerry I hesitated to go because Father seemed worse. Jerry said, "Go ahead and go; I'll be here." So with the assurance that one of us would be near Father, I got on one of those trains crowded with servicemen and headed for Texas. One week after my arrival, we received a telegram that Father had died. It was July 5, 1943, my friend Helen Hale's birthday. Father used to say, "One person dies and another is born to take his place." Now his voice was stilled, but his words of wisdom and understanding would be part of our heritage.

Me, Ken, and Jack, 1946

Chapter XI:

Another Decade of Life

Blessed are the caretakers who even when they feel so exhausted they feel like giving up and never do, but continue and continue to serve to the end. They have their reward. Mother recovered from those sleepless nights and care of Father and lived ten years longer. She saw all five of her grandchildren born and helped with their care. Occasionally she even thought of remarriage, but always thought better of it, especially when a "city" man would say he had always wanted to live in the country. She thought, "Yes. You want to enjoy the clean country air and I can do all the work. Nix on that!" So while she leisurely saw what her options were, she began doing things. She knitted wool helmet liners for the Red Cross to send to servicemen stationed in cold climates, she rented rooms, and even rented out one of the four garages to a company that painted cars. Cars had to last forever in those days since war machines like jeeps and tanks were rolling off the assembly lines instead of black Chevrolet sedans, or blue eight-cylinder Hudsons. Two garages were always kept available for my car and Jerry's car when he was at sea, or it was not my week to drive, and one for Mother's guest. It was not smart to leave cars parked on the street at night. The vehicles might be hit since mandated "blackouts" demanded no parking lights, not even house lights without dark shades.

"Blackouts" and camouflage were the order of the day. Our best man, Arthur Heise, was a camouflage artist. One of his local jobs was disguising the Martin Aircraft plant and parking lot. It was cleverly done. Acres and acres of chicken wire covered buildings and parking lots, and then painted to look like trees and fields near the river (Middle River). We often envied Arthur because he remained a civilian while working in his own field on challenging wartime projects. And we envied Clary Plummer, Marie's husband, who also worked at Martin's. He drove a Crosley, and later a tiny Bantam that was always filled with riders who paid for his gas; he always had more gas than he needed. But most of all we envied Cousin

79

Charlie who spent the war years making airplanes while Brother's ships were dodging Japanese planes and German submarines, and Jack was always vulnerable for overseas duty. But Mother, in her wisdom said, "But not everyone can go; someone has to stay home and work." And work they (we) did, often two jobs; our double shifts plus volunteer work.

Slowly, men, except those elderly or disabled (4F) left the teaching profession. Free periods and extracurricular activities disappeared. Our women gym teachers taught boy's gym, mainly track and marching and basketball in winter, and those of us with free periods donned sweatshirts and monitored the girls. I hated the marching drills (never knowing right from left) and could not wait until some student was proficient enough to take over. I remember one of our male math teachers, a Quaker who remained a conscientious objector, and the pressure the older men put on him to enlist saying, "What will you tell your children when they ask you what you did in the war?" I do not remember what he said or what he did, but soon the math department at Towson High School was all women. And I remember student Jimmy Johnson, who for religious reasons would not say the pledge to the flag. If our principal had not been the son of a Baptist minister and told us to be understanding of these important principles, Jimmy might have had a hard time. He was a good student, a sincere believer in a "nation under God." "Under God" came later. Jimmy's denomination was ahead of its time.

Jack and I spent a brief two weeks with Mother and then resumed our own schedules. We went back to Texas on the train and spent the rest of the summer in the garage apartment in McAllen, Texas. McAllen was beautiful, even in the 103-degree heat in the Rio Grande Valley of Texas to which folks from Chicago, tired of frigid winters, retired. In the town itself, everyone had well-watered lawns, and an orange and a grapefruit and a papaya tree, and shrubbery of poinsettias, which was beautiful at Christmas.

In McAllen, Texas, 1943

We were a bit short of money after the furlough earlier and another trip home and back, so I got a job at the local newspaper, *The Valley Evening Monitor*, selling subscriptions and picking up news items, weddings, enlistments, furloughs, and society stuff. The Latin community was always good for a wedding or an enlistment article. I rode the bus for miles, but the long siestas, from 1:00 to 3:00 PM were exhausting since no one talked to you during that time.

Our landlady thought I might get a quick temporary job at the local sewing factory managed by the principal of the town high school. This I did, making cartridge belts for the army. I was a "tacker." I sewed X's to reinforce cartridge pockets. Most of the women were Mexican who, like me, needed a weekly paycheck. Wives of officers on the local airfield had the inspector's positions sewed up, but once a week the manager let me do payroll, a nice break from sewing X's. Summer sped by. There were many interesting free things to do—watch movies on the post, enjoy Sunday evening supper with families, swim in a pool with a high dive at a nearby club, and take trips across the border into Mexico. If we had had a bit more money we could have spent a weekend in Monterey, a lovely mountain retreat, but we had to be content with Brownsville and Matamoras, especially since we had to go by bus or hitchhike. Hitchhiking was an art. Many folks picked up a soldier and his girl going to the pool, and we always promised to pick up the first soldier or couple who needed a ride when we got home. And we always did a soldier-to-soldier favor.

And then there were Sundays. We were always homesick on Sunday so we went to a different church each week. The United Methodist Church was the biggest and most impressive. The Baptist Church, which held Sunday evening services on their beautiful lawn, had the best speaker. The Lutheran Church we skipped because "What did Luther reform from?" But the Christian Church, an interdenominational church, was the friendliest. They served communion in the pews, each turning to another with the statement, "The body of Christ, and the blood of Christ," and immediately you, a stranger, were indeed part of the community. Now we felt we had Sunday organized. Mother was as good about letter writing as I was. I wrote in English and she wrote in Czech, that way we could dash off a weekly missive with not too much effort, and we both received mail regularly. When September approached and school was about to start, I packed my bags and my new social security card (starting with 451–Texas), got on the train, and headed home.

Home had changed. I realized it was harder to leave Jack this time and sadder to realize that I would not have Father to spar with and bring cigarettes to anymore. Suddenly, Father was not ill and tired and weak and old and weighed down by war's (man's) inhumanity to man. At peace now, he was free to be an idea man, exchanging ideas with the great and the peaceful. Mother was free now too. She could mingle with people, go to the movies, haunt linen shops on Lexington Street, and admire the cutwork and fine embroidered scarves and pillowcases. She enjoyed taking short trips and staying overnight with me, or having Ella over, who loved her so much. Velma came to her house and they danced to the Czech waltzes and polkas. We all went to the theater to see Ethel Barrymore in *How Green Was My Valley* and to one of those Pushkin plays with Russian dancing. Mother confided that for a long time she would be outside doing something and would run indoors to tell Father about it and then realize he was not there anymore. She would say, "When I feel as though the house is going to fall down on me I run away, and being enough of a 'people person,' I always have someplace to run." People were Mother's salvation.

The year of 1943 dragged. Boys who plowed fields at night fell asleep in class. There were frequent air raid drills, and everyone sat on the floors in the corridors; taps were blown often, and some of our best students and leaders were killed in the war. Every teacher became a counselor to someone. I remember writing a letter of condolence to a student whose gentle brother was killed: "We must not let this happen again, this senseless bloodshed." And just what could I do about it? I spent the Christmas holidays with Jack at the Casa de Palmas Hotel in McAllen in endless discussions.

The winter train trip was beautiful if you could block out the vision of all those sailors packed in those cars at night even though your seatmate was a woman traveling to spend a few precious days with her husband about to go overseas. When morning finally came, the palm trees silhouetted against the brightening sky was a sight equal only to the citrus groves, yellow grapefruit followed by orange oranges blending with deeper orange tangerines—tree ripe! What a remarkable sight at Christmas! And tangerines, those special Christmas stocking treats that accented the yellows and the gold on green trees. The room at the hotel was a welcome sight … a tiny Christmas tree with gifts all around.

This time of year was the peak of citrus harvest, and we saw it all. The government bought the complete harvest. Growers tested the fruit for sugar content to determine ripeness, and then shook the trees to drop the fruit. They shipped the ripe fruit to a juice factory and crated the less than ripe fruit for later consumption. Some oranges went to storage sheds, were put through a dye bath, and stamped "color added." It was fun to watch this process. Tomatoes were picked, juiced, dehydrated and powdered, and became part of a soldier's "C" rations. We saw everything here, but knew nothing about this war we were part of.

Being in for the duration and never knowing when one would ship out was disheartening. Well, we would not wait any longer. When Jack made the rank of Staff Sergeant, and I finished the school year, we decided we would start our family. We had waited long enough; this war would never end! And so it was we determined no more tenants would live in our section of the Sue Creek house. Come 1945 we would live there ourselves. June 1944 brought D-Day and many gold stars appeared in windows. So many bodies washed ashore, so many of our generation, now dead heroes.

When the school year ended, I announced my decision to resign from teaching. "You don't have to do that," Reade Corr, the school principal said. "Wait until you see what happens." After all, Reade and Mary had been married for two years already, and they still had no children. "Don't resign in June," Reade repeated. But no, I had my mind made up, I would resign and Jack and I *would* start our family. After all, we had to replace the dead, my father, and those young people for whom that bugle kept blowing.

Christmas in South Carolina, painting pine cones for ornaments, 1944

The Army Air Corps had again transferred Jack, this time to South Carolina. So at the end of June 1944, we gave up the apartment on Lanvale Street, moved our furniture to the shore, packed our portable household items in the 1939 Chevrolet sedan, even our bikes, told everybody our plans, and drove away. We found a place to live on a cotton plantation in Rembert, South Carolina, run by a widow whose son attended Clemson University. A family of blacks did the field-work, one of whom had risen to "share cropper." Aunt Sally was the matriarch, Willie was the sharecropper, John who had six children, and Walter and Albert lived with Aunt Sally. All had small houses on the plantation with a garden and chickens and a pig or two, but they worked for Mrs. Watkins—planting, chopping, and picking cotton. The plantation had horses, cows, pigs, chickens, and a smokehouse. Food was plentiful, and the lifestyle experience was great. In no time, we swapped PX cigarettes for sugar coupons with John, who had more sugar stamps than he could afford to use. Two horses would ride, and with a little help from Albert and Walter, we were all soon galloping over the plantation road and wooden bridge to Mrs. Getha's house.

Albert and Walter rode our bikes to their church sometimes. We were a good southern family. They liked us and we liked them. Even Jack's sister came to visit us. But things did not always go according to schedule. All during June, July, and August, there was no sign of "Junior." It would be a boy; I just knew it. You know boys were always first, besides this one would replace Father, or one of those wonderful young men who died prematurely. Mother thought I was being impatient and Jack thought that maybe I needed to go home for a while. After all, I was accustomed to going back to teaching school about this time. So I returned home for a week or two, but Junior was already on his way. It was an easy pregnancy, no morning sickness, or unusual discomfort, but the uncertainty of war raged on. One time the Army Air Corps placed Jack on alert, and he took me home before reporting to duty. Mother had repapered our apartment with the help of her new/old friend, and I settled down to wait.

Marie and Clary Plummer had their first baby on December 22, 1944, so Marie was a good companion to have in the house. Mother lived close by. Things looked good, but Jack's orders were canceled, and I decided to return to South Carolina and be with him, only this time not to the plantation, but to share a small house with another army couple who had a child, Sparky, born on the Fourth of July. It was a nice living arrangement and the town of Summerville, unlike Charleston, was friendly and helpful to military folks. Mother did not want me to go, reminding me that Jack might get orders to leave for overseas again and leave me stranded. I knew better. Military prenatal care was good and cheap and military folks supported each other.

Suddenly on May 8, 1945, the war with Germany was over. Our first child, Kenneth Usher Mowll, was born in the Port of Embarkation Hospital in Charleston, South Carolina, on Saturday afternoon, May 12—a peacetime baby. Well almost, since peace with Japan did not come until August of that year.

But Mother was right. Jack was off to Fort Pendleton, Massachusetts, exactly one week before Ken was born. We had good care in that military hospital, a full ten days of recovery for our new son and me. Mother's Day, May 13 became a very special day that year. A telegram to Jack announced the news and from there it spread to everyone at home, but somehow Mother got the news last. She did not know I was alone, but I assured her we would be home with her first and only grandson as soon as Jack could get leave. It happened within a month, and Ken went to the graduation of the Towson High School class of '45 (of which I was one of the sponsors).

The rest is less dramatic. After the bomb, and peace with Japan, the duration was over and discharged soldiers came slowly home. Jack arrived early in January

1946. Baby Ken and I had held up Christmas celebrations until Daddy could be here. It was a joyous occasion, and life settled down to what it had been these last four years for those who served at home with shortages and rationing and lack of consumer goods. We chose to give up a little more of our lives for Jack to go back to Hopkins where he had registered for summer school in 1942 just before he was drafted. Returning students had priority; the government paid their tuition and gave them a small monthly allowance. With credit for some of his courses in the military, Jack received his BA in two and a half years (1948) and beat out a PhD in economic geography five years later.

Concurrently with these two academic successes, we had two more children in rapid succession. Nancy was born February 11, 1947, in Sinai Hospital in Baltimore. In contrast to the leisurely ten-day stay in the military hospital in 1945, Nancy and I went home from Sinai after two days because the hospital was so crowded. Some of the mothers were stacked in the old people's retirement section on the top floor, vertical miles away from the nursery. Naturally, the nurses would not carry a new baby through germ-infected floors to her mother who had indicated on the admissions form that she intended to breast-feed the baby! Hospital personnel were not expected to look at information on those forms, let alone read them.

Fortunately, our family doctor, Dr. Mund, believed strongly in breast-fed babies and had me sent home where Mother was on hand caring for twenty-one-month-old Ken and waiting to welcome her new granddaughter. Showing the pink blanket-wrapped baby to Ken, she asked, "What is it Kenny?" He answered sweetly, "A dolly." Speech came quickly to Ken. By his second birthday, he was speaking in sentences. Nancy Lynn Mowll promptly took up the challenge and did everything, walk, and talk, et cetera, just a little faster.

Mother was busy. Two months after Nancy was born, her fourth grandchild, Lynn Frances Matejka was born in Mother's home on April 20, 1947. No hospitals for this one. Hospitals were too crowded, too unsafe. Suppose one couple's child was accidentally mixed up with another couple's child! So it was that their family doctor and his nurse delivered Jerry and Lottie's second daughter at home, just eight years after Rosalie had been born on April 22, 1939. But Jerry and Lottie wanted their own house, and Mother too longed for respite from the dancing and singing Rosie and baby Lynn and the other two grandchildren. Soon they found a big house with a big yard, a garage on treelined Fleetwood Avenue in Overlea, and everyone was happy.

In our two-apartment house on Sue Creek, the Plummers had their third child, a red-haired boy they named David. He too was born at home. After my missed breast-feeding experience at Sinai, Dr. Mund, with the help of his nurse, offered to do a home delivery, and David was born in the middle of the night on December 16, 1947. So the Plummer-Mowll waterfront house now boasted five children; three boys and two girls, a good start for a private kindergarten, with four parents and two grandmothers on call, though not living in that growing nursery.

Since Ken and Nancy were born under not exactly ideal conditions, Ken without a father present and Nancy separated from her mother, and they survived nicely, Jack and I decided to have one more child—a pair and a spare. I figured in my usual "know it all" manner that if you have two children and something happened to one (God forbid) you would have a tendency to smother the remaining one, but if you would have three, the third one would be your challenge. The theory was correct, but the reality was something else.

We confidently ordered another boy because Nancy showed signs at an early age that she could take care of herself. But Roger Douglas turned out to be Marjorie Ann, and she was in no hurry to leave the comfortable womb and join her brother and sister. She was not only a bit late, but was the largest of the three, weighing in at ten pounds. The last three weeks were exhausting for me. I remember mopping the kitchen floor sitting *on* a chair! She finally arrived with a little prodding on March 9, 1949, at Franklin Square Hospital in Baltimore. Well, at least all three children had different hospitals for their safe arrivals.

Ken, Marge, and Nancy, ca. 1951

And so we had a family, but caring for three children under the age of four was a different story. The world did not pause in its spinning to admire our completed family, but seemed to swirl around us at a dizzying pace. Jack, in addition to his academic work for his PhD, became an instructor teaching mainly evening classes. Marie's father passed away and left his house in Middleborough to Marie and her sister, so the Plummers, after much renovation to the old house, decided to make it their home.

Having just paid off our half of the Sue Creek house by cashing in my teacher's pension, we were faced with the prospect of buying out the Plummers portion and moving downstairs and renting out the upper floor to help pay the mortgage on the whole house, now *all* ours. Just about that time, our ten-year-old black Chevrolet sedan began to give out. Mother loaned us money to buy a pretty little blue Renault with the engine in back and the trunk under the hood. Good old mother, now she was our banker in addition to everything else! She took no interest, did not dun us for payment, and we joked when we paid, "Mom, the only reason we're paying you is so we can borrow it again."

The rapid changes, Jack's extra responsibilities at Hopkins, losing the close companionship of Marie's family, having only one car available, and the long, lonely house of childcare took its toll. I spent eight months with Mother, now sixty, pinch-hitting for me full time, and Jack relieving her on weekends. When I could take over again, Mother quickly assumed the care of a child born late in life to a couple whose two older sons were already finishing high school.

Mother not only took care of the youngster, Mac, but also became a valuable friend to the society woman who had birthed the unplanned child. Mother did so many helpful things for Mrs. P, like professionally relining a fur coat. After all, hadn't Mother been the helpmate and assistant to a custom tailor? "Nothing you learn will hurt you," she always said. "You'll always find use for everything you can do well."

For relaxation, Mother enjoyed reading the stacks of Mrs. P's light mystery novels, often reading them faster than Mrs. P, because reading and knowing how to skim "light stuff" in two languages was always a pleasure for Mother.

Brother Jerry shared her interest in reading, buying Horatio Alger books as they came out with his own "earned" money when he was very young. Brother is eighty-three now [this was in 1994] and a few weeks ago he showed me a big bound volume of *Popular Mechanics*, which he said he ordered from the Sears, Roebuck and Company catalog—his first catalog purchase. "To be able to read and write in any language is a treasure you will have forever," Mother used to say. I thought of that when my friend, Marie, suffered a stroke and her speech and small muscle coordination stopped, ending prematurely our philosophical discussions and her delightful letters, which always came no matter where I was at the time.

Mother spent weekends at Jerry's or visiting us. We soon decided that keeping her house was a burden and responsibility we no longer wanted. So we helped her sell the place, taking anything we felt we could use. Since Jack and I had an old chicken house that we used for storage, we took some of the old poultry things like an incubator and several chicken coops, and batteries and cans to store feed in, and bits and pieces of this and that. Some of Mother's special china and glass and memorabilia ended up at Jerry and Lottie's place.

Then Mother did what many would call a very foolish thing. She paid off my mortgage and Jerry's mortgage, which amounted to two-thirds of what she received from the sale of her property. She told us, "If I can't get along with either of you, I will use my money and go to the Czech retirement home in Chicago." And when we protested that she should not give away her money to us she said, "Father always said, 'If you have something to leave your children, give it to them when they *need* it. Don't wait until they beat themselves to death and then leave it to them in your will.' He wants you to have your houses mortgage free." We always knew, Brother and I, that our parents wanted us, carefully nurtured us, and loved us. They loved us even when we did not or could not reciprocate their love.

And now a brief word about the end of that generation. Mother's service to little Mac and Mrs. P was about to end when Mac started kindergarten. It was then that Mother became ill with cancer of the uterus. Doctors at Mercy Hospital thought she was a poor operational risk, but performed the operation anyway. As with Father, I again heard the words, "… six months to live." But remembering Father's six-month prediction lasting seven years, I had mixed feelings about doctors, especially surgeons and their predictions. Were they playing God? This was October, her birth month, and she had come to live with us. Good Dr. Mund, now trying to establish an eye, ear, nose, and throat clinic, accepted Mother as a patient and assured her he could make her comfortable. He said to me privately, "The parent knows, the children know, and each is trying to keep it from each other."

Mother recovered from the operation, and we enjoyed a good Christmas with family intact. In January, Mother said she had always wanted to go to Florida. There was a Czech colony in Miami centered near a popular restaurant where they had excellent food and music and special daily and evening entertainment. A real vacation, a package deal moderately priced. "So, Mom, why don't you go? You know how bad the weather can be here in January," I said.

"But it costs so much money," she countered. I asked her how much she paid for her stay in the hospital—this was before Medicare and Blue Cross—and I suggested she spend the same amount of money for the trip to Florida and call it therapy. She did not really need further persuasion. For once in her life, she would do just what she wanted to do.

Mother in 1953

To Florida she went. She marveled at the palm trees and enjoyed the sunshine and warmth when we were having snow and cold and the trees were bare. She went to the restaurant and enjoyed the food. She enjoyed the welcoming atmosphere, the music, the dancing. She wrote both Brother and me about what a good time she was having. Brother and I saved her last letters, Jerry's written in English, and mine in Czech. Mother returned home in February and lived one more month. We gave her the big bedroom next to the bath, the one that had doors. Baba (Grandma) was very ill, we told Ken, Nancy, and Marge, now eight, six, and four. If her door was open, they could go in and see her. If the door was closed, it meant she was resting, and she needed lots of rest now. On Sundays, Jerry came to spell us a bit, and we took the day off.

We considered putting Mother into a local nursing home, but we knew that she would probably be asleep when we visited, so we decided to take it one day at a time and keep her at home with us. We used the times she was awake to assure her she was safe and surrounded by loved ones trying to repay her for the many times she cared for us even when she herself was too tired to take over. Now it was our turn to be too tired. Mother was an excellent patient and boarder and insisted on buying a side of beef, which she no longer ate, to put in the freezer so we would all have enough food and a good variety of meat cuts. Actually, toward the end, she ate very little, but enjoyed the cold water and other liquids that were always at her bedside. Mother had said if there was any money left when she died, she wanted it divided equally among all five of her grandchildren, and we were to give one hundred dollars to Lillian, Charles and Lillian's daughter.

Mother died the afternoon of March 6, exactly six months after her admittance to the hospital. I was with her when she died and would describe her passing similar to having a baby, uncomfortable but rewarding. We buried Mother on Margie's birthday. My friend Marie baked a beautiful birthday cake. The top was half a doll, the frosted Bundt cake her full skirt. What great things friends often do for each other and their families! My friend Mary Patterson Schmidt's tribute to Mother in her note says it well:

Dear Lib,

I am glad I was able to attend the service for your mother and to be a part of the last good-bye to her. Though embarrassed in a humble sort of way that the flowers and people and service and personal fixing-up were for her, how pleased she truly would have been.

You are no doubt feeling pretty low, and I guess it is a good thing that you have three active children to occupy your time and thought. Margie's fourth birthday will surely stand out in memory. The children all looked so pretty and sweet, and how that too would have pleased Baba.

I'm glad it was not necessary for your mother to endure a longer illness; it would have been most heartrending for you. As it was, I'm sure many an evening that month you fell into bed filled with despair, and weary in body and spirit.

One finds so much to be thankful for, and these things comfort us greatly as time goes on.

Life without your mother will seem most painful for a while, for although she was not in agreement with you always, there was no one who loved you all more, nor proved herself a more helpful friend. God gave you a hardworking, loving mother and her memory will grow ever sweeter as time goes on.

With loving sympathy,

Pat
March 9 [1953]

My friend "Pat" Schmidt

Me and Mom, 2006

Epilogue

Nancy Mowll Mathews

My mother's story about her parents ends with the death of her mother in 1953. I was six years old and remembered my "Baba" very well. She was a warm, stabilizing, and funny presence in a household overrun by young children. I cried at her funeral, although I remember being surprised by the sensation of grief, which was new to me at that time. I could see that my mother was sorry to lose both of her parents so young, and as hard as she tried, she could not convert her in-laws into the wise and worldly protectors that her own parents had been.

My brother, sister, and I grew up in the Sue Creek house that my parents had bought so bravely in the early forties. My mother was successful in duplicating her own childhood for us—we remember the freedom of the countryside since our area of the Maryland shore did not support the massive development that went on all around us. Abundance of homegrown food and regular travel loomed large for us too. And even though we moved to Philadelphia and then to Washington, we managed to keep that beautiful spot for weekends and summers.

My very bold and adventuresome parents encountered their own tragedies. In 1967 we lost my sister Margie in an accident, a life-altering experience that precipitated my parents move back to Sue Creek in sadness. Like many parents who lose children, they could not overcome the shock and divorced in 1974. At the age of sixty-two, my mother, who had previously taken up flying, went to work at the small airport a few miles from the house. She worked there part-time for eleven years. Also in 1985, she sold the Sue Creek house to my father and eventually moved into a condominium in the neighborhood. She had a wide circle of friends from the airport, her golf course, and her church. In 2005, after she had experienced some physical problems, I brought her to live near me in Williamstown, Massachusetts. My brother from Minneapolis visits often with his wife and two children.

My mother's brother Jerry lost his wife, Lottie, in 1985, and soon after, his older daughter, Rosalie. He remained close to his younger daughter, Lynn, and all six of his grandchildren. When he died in 1995, Lynn kept her ties to my mother and us, her only cousins. She is a wonderful correspondent to my mother, as are her two daughters. The Matejkas did not produce a very large family of descendents, but there is intense pride in us all.

What has been their legacy? We have all traveled to the Czech Republic over the years with the typical "descendent of immigrants" curiosity. We find many Czech Americans among our friends without realizing it. But mostly we are nurtured by the stories of our family's past, a living history that is of both personal and worldwide importance. The impact of the greatest migration in world history, that of millions of people coming to the United States in the years around 1900, has yet to be fully comprehended in human terms. The more we can learn of their lives and the families they shaped, the greater will be our understanding of similar events in our future.

About the Authors

Slava Elizabeth Matejka Mowll was born in Baltimore, Maryland, in 1914. She attended local elementary and high schools around Essex, Maryland, and graduated from Goucher College in 1935. She taught math and science at Towson High School in Towson, Maryland, from 1935 to 1944. She married Jack Usher Mowll (born in Cleveland, Ohio, in 1915) and in 1941 had three children. She was active as a volunteer in the school systems of Baltimore County and Haverford, Pennsylvania. Returning to Baltimore, Maryland, in 1967, she was a well-known figure at the Essex Sky Park and at the Rocky Point Golf Course. She has been a longtime member of Hope Lutheran Church in Middleborough. She currently resides in Williamstown, Massachusetts.

Nancy Mowll Mathews is the Eugénie Prendergast Senior Curator of Nine-teenth- and Twentieth-Century Art and Lecturer in Art at the Williams College Museum of Art. She is an art historian specializing in French and American art around 1900. She was born in Baltimore and graduated from Goucher College in 1968. She has her PhD from the Institute of Fine Arts of New York University. She has taught at Randolph-Macon Woman's College from 1977 to 1987 and has been at Williams College since 1988. At Williams, she is the director of the Prendergast Archive and Study Center and teaches in the graduate and under-graduate programs. She is the author of twelve books and organizes numerous major exhibitions that have traveled around the world.

978-0-595-46769-3
0-595-46769-5

www.ingramcontent.com/pod-product-compliance
Lightning Source LLC
Chambersburg PA
CBHW030348290526
45785CB00004B/1654